T0115069

Perpetuating American Greatness after the Fiscal Cliff
Jump Starting GDP Growth, Tax Fairness and Improved Government Regulation

iUniverse books may be ordered through booksellers or by contacting:

iUniverse
1663 Liberty Drive
Bloomington, IN 47403
www.iuniverse.com
1-800-Authors (1-800-288-4677)

ISBN: 978-1-4759-7591-8 (sc)
ISBN: 978-1-4759-7593-2 (hc)
ISBN: 978-1-4759-7592-5 (e)

Library of Congress Control Number: 2013902495

Printed in the United States of America

iUniverse rev. date: 3/11/2013

Contents

Author's Note

The author has been engaged in the private practice of law in New York City for almost 50 years specializing in corporate and securities matters. His clients' needs involved him in a broad range of business, commercial, real estate, tax and trust and estate matters. Although he has had little time to pursue his interests in macroeconomic theory developed while he was a student at Brown University or securities regulation that he studied at Harvard Law School, he has kept current over the years in each of these areas.

He became alarmed by our country's lack of preparedness in dealing with the terrorist acts of 9/11/2001 and the threat which potential future terrorist acts posed to our safety and our economy while we were trying to recover from the economic downturn that followed the bursting of the .com bubble. He wrote and self-published his first book entitled "Homeland Security and Economic Prosperity" in 2003 as an attempt to offer suggestions for strengthening homeland security and improving government regulation of our economy. He watched as we made limited improvements in our homeland security and the GDP appeared to recover largely as a result of our out-of-control banks creating housing and banking bubbles, the collapse of which led us into the Great Recession.

The following chapters review the failures of the politicians of both the Democratic and Republican parties in managing our federal and state governments and in regulating our free market capitalism. They examine the material adverse effects such failures have had on the US economy. They discuss the serious damage caused by our bankers that led to the Great Recession and the events leading to the "Fiscal Cliff" and the currently unacceptable state of our economy. The author suggests steps to be taken to reverse the economic decline and create jobs necessary to grow the GDP and reduce the annual government deficit. He introduces Jump Start America Bonds to encourage our cash rich businesses and wealthy individuals to step up and invest in America. He proposes what he expects will be a controversial new mortgage law and US Mortgage Court to assist the forgotten middle class by permitting the restructuring of most home mortgages on terms that will end the housing crisis and benefit both the borrowers and the lenders. Income and estate tax law modifications are proposed which unlike the tax changes that were adopted in dealing with the Fiscal Cliff are intended to close loopholes and raise revenues without harming economic growth or punishing the taxpayers who were already paying a fair share of their income in taxes.

They also express the author's concerns and recommendations relating to a broad range of matters that have been the subject of national discussion during 2012, including income and estate tax fairness, the jobs problem, the housing crisis and its effect on the middle class, the current state and future of our economy, the Fiscal Cliff, the GDP, the national debt, federal deficits, the effect of the first four years of the Obama Presidency on the US economy, entitlements, Obamacare, federal, state and city debt problems, excessive risk taking and regulation of banks (including the proposal of a federal usury law), the Dodd-Frank legislation, securities and commodities regulation, and the manipulative effects of short selling.

The author discusses the American Taxpayer Relief Act of 2012 which eliminated the most catastrophic elements of the Fiscal Cliff but together with the Obamacare taxes exacerbated our county's economic problems by unfairly taxing families and the productive and job creating members of our society earning between $200,000 and $1,000,000 and failed to address the debt, spending or entitlement issues. The author expresses his concern that dealing with the Fiscal Cliff, government spending and the national debt have distracted our politicians from concentrating on the need to take steps to create jobs and stimulate economic growth.

The author is concerned with the lack of awareness of the public of the dangers facing the American economy. He is particularly concerned with the blind faith of a majority of Americans, including our youngest and minority voters, that President Obama is heading our economy in the right direction despite what they believe to be obstructionist actions being taken by conservative Republicans for political purposes. He is equally concerned that the austerity measures demanded by conservatives Republicans will lead the economy back into a recession. He does not believe that lies and demagoguery used by politicians to mislead the public are appropriate for political debate and is concerned with the failure of the press to expose and confront such wrongful statements.

The author is hopeful that the president's supporters many of whom seem to believe everything he says and get angry when anyone criticizes him will read his suggestions which are offered to assist the president and the conservative opposition alike in resolving the myriad of problems leading to our economic decline so that we can grow our economy and preserve American greatness.

Certain of the author's thoughts are repeated in more than one chapter so that each chapter may be read separately. Although some of the legislative proposals are described in detail, the drafting of the laws is left to congressional staff members.

The factual information referred to has been derived in large part from newspapers, magazines, Internet searches and TV financial news programs during the year and although it is believed by the author to be accurate it has in some cases not been independently verified.

Introduction

As the winter of 2012-2013 and the "Fiscal Cliff" approached, the US remained as the strongest nation in the world. However, over a period of a few decades our great country has witnessed many changes in the manner in which we conduct and regulate free market capitalism. The changes have had a material adverse effect upon our economy and many of our citizens, including a majority of the middle class. The collapse of the housing market and the banking industry during 2008 resulted in our economy incurring devastating multi-trillion dollar losses and the loss of eight million jobs leading to the Great Recession.

Many factors, including trillions of dollars of stimulus spending during the first four years of the Obama administration, have temporarily reversed the decline. However, our GDP has lost years of satisfactory growth with the result that our federal and state governments have had insufficient annual revenues to meet their expenditures leading to excessive and growing debt greatly weakening the economic strength of our country. The unemployed and underemployed including young people entering the job market face limited opportunities to pursue the American dream of success.

We will explore what has gone wrong in our cherished country at all levels of government and suggest new directions to pursue to rejuvenate our economy and preserve American greatness. In doing so, we will examine (i) why the failed Obama stimulus package, which largely relied upon standard Keynesian spending and tax relief for consumers, has greatly increased the national debt but failed to create an acceptable number of jobs despite TARP adopted under the leadership of George W, Bush and QE1, QE2 and QE3 (and other actions) taken by the Federal Reserve Board (the "Fed"), and (ii) why a change back to a focus on supply side economics would not create enough stimulus and would likely result in further unacceptable increases in the national debt.

We cannot afford another four years pursuing the same failed policies and add another five to ten trillion dollars to the national debt. We must find a way to substantially increase the rate of growth of the GDP and reduce the rate of growth of the national debt before we are engulfed by the looming entitlement crisis. Unless we do so we are going to have to print a massive amount of dollars that will lead to a high rate of inflation and a decline in the value of the dollar.

THE US ECONOMY

The Fiscal Cliff

In December 2012 we faced a situation where existing federal tax and spending laws with sunset provisions or delayed effectiveness had created the Fiscal Cliff that was set to occur at the end of 2012. The Fiscal Cliff included the elimination of all of the Bush tax cuts, the substantial increase in the income tax on dividends, the ending of the reduced payroll deductions, the ending of the alternative minimum tax fix to adjust for inflation, the increase in the capital gains tax, the end of the doctor Medicare compensation fix, the reduction in the term of extended unemployment benefits, the elimination of tax relief from short sales, the automatic increases in the gift and estate taxes, various other tax and spending laws which require annual action, and the ridiculously dangerous sequestration law, which requires reductions in defense and discretionary spending proposed by President Obama and passed by Congress in 2011 in response to demands by conservative Republicans that US government spending be reduced.

The Fiscal Cliff should be looked at as a potentially devastating man made economic storm that was approaching our economy. President Obama orchestrated the Fiscal Cliff by arranging the postponement of the sunset provisions of the Bush tax cuts and other matters so that the negative impact of each of the items that made up the Fiscal Cliff would occur after the election. If Congress had done nothing automatic tax increases and spending cuts combined with the new Obamacare taxes effective in 2013 would have caused a severe downturn in the GDP, and the national debt that might have declined for a brief period would have risen precipitously.

Conservative Republicans clung to the argument that they would not approve individual income tax rate increases, which they claimed would harm small businesses and be counter-productive. Some less conservative Republicans sought to compromise by offering tax increases for taxpayers earning over a million dollars or by reducing deductions of higher income taxpayers, which might have had a similar result. Although both parties seemed to agree that sequestration as previously enacted by Congress should be eliminated, Republicans were insisting on different cuts in government expenditures that they claimed would reduce the federal deficit. They also were insisting on a modification in entitlements to avert future catastrophic cost increases. Republicans might have been better able to please their base by allowing all the Bush tax cuts to expire and then arguing when the negotiations commenced early in 2013 to reinstate them that they were only compromising on tax reductions for the poor and the middle class.

The President was insisting on his proposed tax increase on families earning over $250,000 that he treated as if it was a panacea, but which was almost meaningless. He claimed (which was disputed by Republicans) that he had made a trillion dollars of spending reductions and was considering others as well as entitlement reform. He ignored the other negative aspects of the Fiscal Cliff. He doesn't appear to care about the growing national debt and apparently believed that if he got his tax increase the economy will resume its slow growth and housing will continue to recover. He and his advisors seem to favor shared mediocrity. He succeeded in postponing discussions about adjusting or reducing entitlements or discretionary spending which Republicans deem important until after the Fiscal Cliff was avoided. Some Republicans believed they could control spending and the national debt ceiling after dealing with the Fiscal Cliff because of their control of the House of Representatives. They seem to have forgotten that they embarrass themselves every time they even talk about creating a situation that might cause the US to default in a debt payment.

Rather than encourage a settlement by members of Congress President Obama chose to take his case to the public claiming that Republicans were willing to cause a tax increase for 98% of Americans to prevent a small tax increase on the rich. He relied on the liberal press to encourage capitulation by the Republicans that he succeeded in obtaining. As adopted the inappropriately named American Taxpayer Relief Act of 2012 incorporated in large part the tax proposals that were demanded by President Obama. Many of our rich taxpayers would not have objected to the substantial tax increases if they believed that they represented a solution to our country's ills. However, the tax changes as adopted will not significantly reduce the federal deficit.

Congress at the same time approved a two-month extension for dealing with the sequestration requirement and postponed action on debt and entitlement issues and the need to increase the national debt ceiling. We do not know how our dysfunctional Congress will deal with those issues. Our politicians seem to have forgotten about the need to create jobs and grow our economy.

The prior rates of taxation and spending had been baked into the system and coupled with other stimulus efforts had resulted in only a minor upturn in the GDP. Although the worst potential effect of the Fiscal Cliff that would have resulted in the largest tax increase in our nation's history was avoided many of the negative aspects of the Fiscal Cliff as modified to reduce their severity were permitted to take effect. They together with the upcoming debate about entitlement and spending reductions and the debt ceiling coupled with the effects of Obamacare and Dodd Frank are going to slow the growth of the economy or put it back into recession. Businesses may be encouraged by a reasonably satisfactory resolution of the Fiscal Cliff but it is difficult to envision how any resolution would have produced a significant number of jobs and led to significant economic growth.

Our business leaders generally favor tax reductions coupled with greater spending cuts. Various economists and businessmen have proposed the adoption of a form of the previously proposed and rejected Simpson-Bowles legislation, which relies in part on reduced tax rates and reduced deductions (including the home mortgage deduction) as a way to resolve the Fiscal Cliff.

Dealing with the Fiscal Cliff proved to be a distraction from the resolution of our major economic problem of insufficient GDP growth. Although President Obama had asked for a small stimulus program to be added in conjunction with the resolution of the Fiscal Cliff neither party has a program to significantly grow the economy. Republicans are insisting on reducing spending and modifying entitlements to bring future costs under control. They do not seem to understand that only by inducing substantial job growth will we get the US economic engine started to grow the GDP and reduce the annual US government deficit. Increasing tax rates and legislating austerity measures without creating jobs will within a short time frame increase, not decrease the deficit.

The devastating losses caused by hurricane Sandy, coupled with the retrenchment in hiring and capital spending by businesses during the last half of 2012 because of concerns about the election results, the approaching Fiscal Cliff, the anticipated costs of Obamacare and the response to the Dodd-Frank legislation, the problems in Europe and China's slowing economy, caused an economic slowdown as the Fiscal Cliff approached and was discussed. On the other hand, the cleanup, repairs, replacements and reconstruction related to hurricane Sandy that will follow are going to create a large number of construction jobs and auto replacements to be financed in large part by US government funds and private insurance proceeds and provide a material stimulus to our economy.

Nevertheless, despite the potential dire consequences of inaction relative to the Fiscal Cliff the stock market did not react negatively prior to the election. The liberal financial press, not wanting to harm the President's election chances, said almost nothing about the Fiscal Cliff prior to the election. Apparently investors were unaware of the approaching problem or were waiting for the election results and felt that the lame duck Congress would in the best interest of our country rise to the occasion and deal quickly and effectively with the problem or that the problem would be resolved quickly and retroactively by the next Congress. Possibly our short term investors believed they could get out instantly as soon as they sensed a decline has begun and many of them did after the election. The failure of the stock market to decline as the Fiscal Cliff approached may have removed a sense of urgency for our politicians to deal with the problem until we actually went over the Fiscal Cliff for a few hours.

Profit taking to avoid paying new Obamacare taxes and increased capital gains rates in 2013 and the declaration of special dividends by corporations to avoid expected higher dividend rates took place before the end of 2012. Such actions generated extra 2012 tax revenues that will reduce the 2012 federal deficit but will be offset by reduced tax revenues in 2013.

While Congress is preoccupied by the postponed sequestration problem and other issues relating to government spending our national debt is skyrocketing. We watch our sluggish economy hoping for an upturn but fearing a downturn that might lead us into a recession or a depression.

Unless there is an unexpected increase in consumer spending or business investment and hiring or Congress takes steps to stimulate job creation, our economy will at best limp along with annual federal deficits of over a trillion dollars. The middle class will continue to suffer and the entitlement problems that lurk in the background will become more imminent and difficult to resolve.

President Obama made new demands for an agreement to raise the US debt ceiling as part of the resolution of the Fiscal Cliff but let the issue be postponed to be part of the discussions concerning spending and entitlements. He correctly argues that we already incurred the debt and that we cannot default on our obligations. The Republicans should agree to extend the national debt ceiling and argue that they want to reduce excessive and wasteful spending and bring entitlements under control to avoid future increases in the debt ceiling. However, for the reasons stated herein they should not be looking to prevent spending needed to stimulate the economy.

There turned out to be a consensus to let the withholding tax cut reductions expire because such reductions reduce Social Security contributions which if continued indefinitely would have led to arguments that if we are contributing less toward Social Security we should expect to receive reduced benefits. Reducing withholding taxes should never have been used as a way to stimulate the economy.

American consumers have been expressing increased confidence in the US economy. Prior to the election most of them knew nothing about the Fiscal Cliff. They listened to the President's demands that we continue the Bush tax cuts for the 98% of families earning less than $250,000 and did not anticipate any tax increases would affect them. They listened to the president demagogue about the rich paying a little bit more and thought that would solve all of our economic problems. They were shocked when they received their first paycheck in 2013 and found out that their withholding taxes have been increased. Most of them didn't realize that the increase merely reversed the temporary reduction they had received two years earlier.

The president may believe that if the economy goes into recession in 2013, the national debt is increased by a trillion dollars or more and unemployment rises, the Republicans will be blamed and unable to withstand his demands for further tax increases on the rich and substantial stimulus spending to create jobs regardless of its effect on the federal deficit or the national debt so that the US economy will be in an upturn before the end of his four year term. He obviously has a plan to have the Democrats regain control of the House of Representatives at the midterm elections in 2014.

The Great Recession

Beginning before the turn of the century, our banks, under intense political pressure principally from Democrats and civil rights organizations, began to provide mortgages to unqualified home buyers. Such practice coupled with the ability to sell the mortgages to FNMA and Freddie Mac led to the creation of subprime mortgages, which over time generated an excess demand for housing and the housing bubble.

The banks leveraged their mortgage operations by making high risk loans secured by mortgages and used the mortgages to collateralize all types of low grade mortgage backed securities ("MBSes"), which they fraudulently sold as AAA securities based on ratings they bought from conflicted rating agencies. In their thirst to increase short-term income to be awarded personal bonuses and other benefits, bank executives originated and sold securities that created undo risks for their shareholders and were often contrary to the interest of their customers. They also sought to enhance their profits from proprietary trading and hedging of all types of securities including newly created complex derivatives bearing excessive risks that most of them did not fully understand. The executives of our banks and investment banks were gambling with stockholders' and creditors' money seeking to earn egregiously excessive compensation. They developed highly complex computer programs and hired and highly compensated bright traders to manage the risks.

Bank executives used discretionary accounting practices to overvalue assets and understate the need for reserves for losses. This allowed them to overstate current earnings to enable them to earn substantial personal rewards supposedly based on performance. Short-term investors do not generally object to the payment of excess compensation based on performance. They may benefit from increased earnings even if based on fraudulent accounting when the stock price rises and they realize short-term profits.

If highly leveraged banks make or purchase high-risk loans or investments without establishing appropriate reserves, there is a high probability that circumstances will occur that cause them to report substantial losses when management's unrealistic estimates prove to be unjustified. In valuing their mortgages and MBSes, many bankers relied on the insane premise that because of inflation, housing prices would go up indefinitely or at least would not decline in value no matter how overpriced housing became. Bankers also relied on late fees, resetting interest rates and prepayment penalties to generate profits.

By failing to require adequate reserves, our regulators and the accounting industry (which has generally carefully sought ways to avoid liability for erroneous or fraudulent estimates appearing in their clients' financial statements) were enablers. Our banks overvalued the MBSes they sold and continued to overvalue them and ignored the risk of loss after some of the mortgages included in the MBSes began to default when teaser loans were not refinanced. The bankers reported large profits and received large bonuses and cashed in their stock based compensation.

When the housing and mortgage bubble collapsed, major banks became insolvent, lending froze, housing prices and the home construction industry went into steep decline, mortgages went into default, MBSes and other securities prices collapsed and federal, state and local tax revenues plummeted.

At the time the housing and banking bubbles burst, most of our large banks were heavily involved in buying and selling all types of unregulated complex derivative securities, which were subject to unknown or ignored risks or counterparty risks. They were overleveraged with clearly overvalued assets. We have learned painfully that when our country's largest banks that were leveraged at 20 to 1 or more had their investments decline in value by more than 10% they become hopelessly insolvent.

When major banks collapsed, our country was suddenly in the Great Recession, resulting in a precipitous downturn in the GDP, thousands of business closings and the loss of more than 8 million jobs. It affected the financial viability of not only our banks but also many of our citizens and businesses. In a short time beginning in 2008, US households lost more than 15 trillion dollars of wealth nationwide. Most of our previously ineptly governed and over extended states lost a significant portion of their income tax and real property tax revenues and were forced to cut back on spending, including the need to reduce public employee payrolls and infrastructure spending.

Fortunately, Treasury Department officers appointed by President George W. Bush, who had blundered by letting Lehman Brothers go bankrupt, rescued our banking system from potential insolvency by getting Congress to reluctantly approve TARP. On the other hand, our overleveraged banks still faced devastating losses from their overvalued assets and from their prior mortgage related activities. The Fed promptly adopted QE1 and then QE2 and QE3 over a period of more than four years for among other reasons to shore up the banks' balance sheets.

The Great Recession was much different than previous recessions after World War II. It had little or no effect on some sectors of our economy while devastating others, such as banking, housing and auto production. Many of our citizens and businesses prospered or were only marginally affected while many large and small businesses closed and workers lost their jobs and everything they had. GM and Chrysler, which were struggling to survive prior to the Great Recession became insolvent and required massive governmental assistance to remain in business.

Despite the Great Recession, a small percentage of Americans employed as corporate executives, investment managers or entertainers or who invested in certain hi-tech, internet or social networking entities, short sellers who benefitted from the banking and housing collapse and the Great Recession, or investors who bought commodities, bonds, businesses or equities at the bottom of the markets have been able to amass large fortunes aggregating hundreds of millions or billions of dollars. The net worth of the middle class has been decimated. Too many people are jobless or working in low paying dead-end jobs and losing hope of ever achieving the American dream by working hard to purchase a home and improve the lives of their families. The income spread between high income and medium and low-income families is widening.

Economists look to the growth of the GDP and determine that the Great Recession has ended and that we are enjoying modest growth. However, the growth was fueled by tax reductions and government deficit spending and will probably not prove sustainable now that the Fiscal Cliff has passed and some of the stimulus has been removed. We must take steps to insure that the Great Recession does not return.

Current Economic Conditions

Many US based corporations have strong balance sheets and are growing, but the US economy has been greatly weakened and no longer dominates the world economy. The latest economic data shows that we are reporting small, unsatisfactory increases in the Gross Domestic Product (GDP) and that an inadequate number of good paying jobs are being created. We continue to have a large number of wealthy individuals getting richer, a decline in middle class income and a growing number of families living in poverty but not hungry and with limited comforts as a result of the receipt of government handouts. President Obama and the Democrats have made it clear that they want to use the Great Recession as an excuse to further redistribute wealth and steer our economy toward European type socialism.

History books will show that the principle blame for the Great Recession should be placed on bankers, investment bankers, politicians, both liberal and conservative, a large number of people connected with the housing industry and individuals who suffered some of the greatest losses because they bought homes on unrealistic payment terms or that they knew or should have known they couldn't afford or borrowed the equity in their homes to finance their profligate living expenses.

The jobs picture is worse than it appears. Many millions of good paying jobs that helped the US develop a strong middle class have disappeared before and during the Great Recession while our population and the number of prospective workers has grown. Approximately 23 million Americans are unemployed, underemployed or have given up looking for work and the number is increasing because we are not creating enough additional jobs to employ the young people who graduate from college or high school or seek to join the work force each year.

There have been some positive developments around the world, and many of our manufacturing and service companies have benefited from globalization. China and other developing nations played a vital role in preventing the Great Recession from further deteriorating into a depression with consequences that would have been comparable to the Great Depression of the 1930's. Where would we be without the demand for exports to the BRIC countries (Brazil, Russia, India and China) and other developing nations and their suppliers of products such as food, machinery and equipment and raw materials?

Built in safeguards, such as tax loss carry-backs and carry-forwards, unemployment insurance, the wealth effect of the stock market recovery and inventory restocking, played an important role in at least temporarily stemming the downturn. Almost all of the new jobs in the past four years have been created by private industry with help from the Fed, but with little help from or despite the interference of the Obama administration. Our international corporations rapidly expanded in the developing world and added new jobs for Americans both at home and abroad. Domestic jobs were created in connection with the sale of machinery and equipment, food and raw materials, including coal, to the developing world. New high technology products from companies like Apple and the dynamic expansion of wireless communications and the Internet, including the development of social networking, have created a substantial number of new good jobs many of which, as in the .com era, are with entities that will not succeed. Meanwhile, employers are continuing to take advantage of automation efficiencies to reduce staff and increase profitability.

The middle class has been decimated by job losses and the housing collapse that has caused home prices to decline by trillions of dollars. Our economy is stagnant and faces strong headwinds. Although we have avoided major terrorist attacks upon our homeland after 9/11/2001, terrorist cells are growing in many places and pose a growing threat to our lives and our economy. We may be better prepared to prevent the next terrorist attack but since we haven't seriously been tested and we always learn from hindsight how ineffectively our government agencies operate we must continually focus on enhancing our capabilities for dealing with a major terrorist act anywhere in our country at any time. The recent events in the Newtown CT grade school and our Libyan embassy demonstrate how difficult it is to prevent acts of terrorism organized within or outside our borders.

Most politicians, commentators and a large number of economists do not even understand what we should be striving for with respect to the national debt and the federal deficit. It is not the aggregate size of the national debt or the annual federal deficit that is the problem, but their rate of growth as compared to the rate of growth of the GDP. A rapidly growing GDP will generate the tax revenues we need to meet our US government obligations, including the national debt, and to permit the states to meet their obligations. The $16 trillion national debt is a staggering amount. It would have been much lower and less of a problem if our GDP was 20% higher as it might have been if we had avoided or if we had made a stronger recovery from the Great Recession. The national debt is going to grow much larger unless we find a way to stimulate the economy. Federal tax revenues have returned to pre-2008 levels while federal spending has increased leaving us with trillion dollar deficits for the foreseeable future.

The housing market remains a cause of hardship for homeowners and a major stumbling block to an economic recovery. Prior to the collapse in housing prices and the Great Recession that followed, housing was the most important asset of the middle class and many other Americans. Real estate taxes and filing fees, which increased each year as the prices of homes rose, were a major source of revenue for states, counties and cities.

As a result of the collapse of the housing bubble, millions of homeowners, or about 30% of all homeowners, are living in homes with underwater mortgages and many of them face foreclosure. Many of the job losses during the Great Recession were suffered by members of the middle class that was also among the group hardest hit by the housing collapse. As a result, the middle class has witnessed a major decline in wealth.

Very little has been done to help distressed homeowners. Instead, the housing market was permitted to fester and home prices fell in many parts of the country by more than 35% following the collapse of the housing bubble despite the fact that the consumer price index during the period rose by approximately 10%. The American dream of becoming middle class by finding a good job, buying a home and having it increase in value over time due to normal inflation, as your family grew while you made your mortgage payments and invested in home improvements, has turned into a nightmare.

The housing crisis will be alleviated by a rebound in housing prices, which has begun, but cannot end for many years unless we find a way to deal with underwater mortgages. Having the bank foreclose or gain possession via a short sale and then resell the home to an investor at a low price to be held for rental or resale is not an acceptable solution. Too many families would be destroyed financially and the banks would not be minimizing their losses. We built too many homes during the housing bubble, many of which are occupied by people who can't afford them. Now, we must find a way to make a significant number of such homes affordable to the people currently living in them.

The current pain being felt by the middle class, and Americans who have been driven out of the middle class, is unfair and inexcusable. A large percentage of the unemployed or underemployed seek good paying jobs. The Obama administration and the Democrats have not acted to stimulate the creation of good paying jobs for those who want to work. Instead they have promoted increased welfare benefits, which are creating a growing class of Americans who are giving up looking for work or accepting low paying, part time or off the books jobs and are satisfied living in large part off the efforts of others. The development poses a long-term threat to the survival of American capitalism.

Talk by President Obama during the election campaign about punishing companies that ship jobs overseas and giving incentives to companies creating domestic jobs was designed to appeal to the unemployed and particularly blue collar workers but disregards the existence of a world-wide economy and the difficulties of determining if a job has been brought home. It is likely to meet resistance in Congress and be forgotten. Some businesses are considering bringing some production back home, but that will come to fruition when they consider it economically viable to do so.

There is a risk that unrest will develop as a result of a backlash from taxpayers to increasing welfare dependency. We must remember that only a few years ago under President Clinton we focused on creating jobs and reducing welfare by passing a law adding a work requirement for welfare. President Obama has made it clear that he will violate that law by not enforcing the work requirement.

We should note, moreover, that the last surplus achieved under President Clinton did not occur because of sound economic growth, but because he served during the .com bubble which led to unreasonably high stock prices for technology companies and to the collection of substantially increased income and capital gains taxes. The .com bubble resulted in large part from the failure to regulate fraudulent and pie-in-the-sky sales projections for the .com start-up companies recklessly promoted by brokers. The .com bubble burst and the NASDAQ average peaked much higher than current levels in the last year of his term. Fortunately for President Clinton's reputation, the downturn in the US economy didn't take place until after he left office. It became a problem for incoming President G.W. Bush, who, like all presidents, made mistakes, but gets blamed by President Obama and the Democrats for everything wrong with the US economy, including the problems caused by or contributed to by Democrats.

Our cost conscious businesses run by executives whose excessive compensation is justified by their ability to cut costs and increase short term profits (often through layoffs) do not currently create enough jobs in the aggregate to prevent unacceptable levels of unemployment nationwide even during an upturn in the business cycle. Our housing market is in disarray. Our banking system is a national disgrace. The losses that our banks have fraudulently and recklessly incurred have jeopardized our economy. Our investment banks, hedge funds, private equity entities, wealth management advisors and traders have become dominant investment forces that have been poorly regulated. They have from time to time disrupted and caused erratic movements in our securities markets causing systemic risk. Many of our Congressmen seem more interested in receiving campaign funding from special interest groups and fooling the public to get reelected than in passing laws to properly regulate and improve our economy.

One of the exciting aspects of free-market capitalization is that wealth wisely invested produces wealth and creates jobs. Seed money entities have funded thousands of technology and Internet companies and have reaped billions of dollars of profits as a reward for their early investments. Corporations earning 5 to 10% on their capital each year generate cash flow and earnings to expand their operations except to the extent that they add it to their capital, use it to reduce debt, pay dividends or redeem their stock. A growing population should lead to an increased demand for products and services. However, when free market capitalism goes amuck as in recent years and causes loss of wealth it often leads to the further destruction of wealth and loss of jobs.

One of the negative aspects of free-market capitalism is that when an investment is successful and yields a substantial profit it often attracts investors and speculators who, seeking profits, drive up the price of similar types of investments to exorbitant levels, causing a bubble. Wealth can be created during a bubble, but some of the wealth is not real because of the inflated prices that buyers are willing to pay during the term of the bubble with the expectation of selling at even higher prices. When the bubble collapses, as in the case of the recent housing, mortgage and banking bubbles, the excess value disappears and the value of the underlying assets often declines below what would be the expected fair market value and continues downward as wealth is destroyed.

Our economy has from our nation's formation been the subject of periods of prosperity and recession, and our Congress with the benefit of leadership from our then serving president has taken steps to attempt to promote its long term growth. However, our recent Congresses and regulators under the leadership of both parties have lost their way. They have failed to regulate, even encouraged, banking, investment and corporate management practices that are destroying American greatness. If they had adequately regulated our banking system, the Great Depression would not have occurred. Dodd-Frank passed without bipartisan support is an attempt to add new regulations for the financial community and is at best a weak start in trying to regulate a banking system out of control and in disarray. It has caused great confusion, discouraged lending and leaves the banking system vulnerable to the same type of lending practices that spawned the mortgage bubble.

Our federal government faces entitlement and debt problems. Many of our state and local governments facing revenue shortfalls and rapidly increasing healthcare and retirement obligations are virtually insolvent and reducing employment and infrastructure construction spending. We must get our federal and state governments, private industry and wealthy investors to work together to create a sufficient stimulus to jump-start the economy and keep it moving forward to fuel a sustainable recovery. Our economy has the potential for substantial growth. Our autos have an average age of 12 years and we are selling only 14.5 million cars annually. We have years of family formations that have outpaced home purchases.

President Obama, despite squandering $830 billion of stimulus funds, takes credit for the modest cyclical recovery from the Great Recession. The five million jobs he erroneously claims he produced are clearly inadequate to provide jobs for young people seeking to join the work force each year as well as those who lost their jobs. Such number of jobs even if they had been created from his efforts would be extremely disappointing when compared to the number of jobs added during previous post recession recoveries. Moreover, if we examine his claims relating to job creation we find that he gives no credit to the Fed, which believes that its actions have added over two million of the jobs. Nor does he give any credit to businesses, which have created millions of jobs despite the many obtrusive laws and regulations Democrats rushed to pass during his first two years as president. His continuous deficit spending has added over $6 trillion to the national debt. After deducting the jobs created independently of his stimulus efforts including those added from the cleanup, repair and rebuilding following weather related disasters, including hurricane Irene in 2011, those created by the oil and gas industry despite his interference and the loss of public sector jobs his stimulus spending has added few jobs at an outrageous cost for each one. Our national debt has grown excessively during President Obama's first term, not only from the cost of his failed stimulus efforts, but also from the failure of such stimulus efforts to substantially increase the GDP. We have learned that stimulus efforts that focus on safety net payments do not generate jobs or tax revenues or have a meaningful multiplier effect on GDP growth.

Our monthly unemployment rate as published by the DOL using its own flawed definition of unemployment remained above 8% for most of 2012. Actual unemployment exceeds 15% and is rising when we add the underemployed and those people who have accepted lesser jobs, have given up looking for a job or are among the five million people (a suspiciously high number) who have qualified for disability since President Obama took office. It is even higher if we count young people who could be working part time. The unemployment numbers also ignore an increase in the number of college graduates who have never been employed and have elected to stay in graduate schools because they can't find acceptable jobs.

A large percentage of college graduates who can't find jobs will inevitably default on their college loans or will have to seek and obtain relief from the government. Many young people have given up trying to find employment or do not want to accept a lesser dead-end job and are getting by living at home or by receiving a variety of available welfare payments such as food stamps, whose use has been expanded by more than 15 million people under President Obama. Many of our inner city poor, including high school students who would benefit from part-time work can't find employment of any kind and are being induced into joining gangs, leading to an increase in crime.

Looking back to the late 1990s, we find that we suffered economic downturns beginning with the collapse of the .com bubble and the attacks of 9/11/2001. When the economy thereafter turned and accelerated upward, we thought that prosperity had returned. How wrong we were. The housing bubble was financed by the issuance of low grade and in many cases worthless mortgages which banks were anxious to give to non-credit worthy borrowers because they knew they could dispose of them to the US government-backed entities or to unsuspecting buyers.

Banks also promoted the use of homes as ATM machines leaving a large number of homeowners with mortgages that totaled a very high percentage of the over-valued equity in their homes. The reduced percentage of equity in homes created a credit risk that was compounded by the banks' promoting the use of credit cards with excessive credit limits, which they offered to college students and which they encouraged consumers to use by mass advertising and solicitations offering what they call rewards but which the consumer pays for indirectly.

We have discovered that free market capitalism when not properly regulated encourages excessive risk taking, fraud and manipulation by banks, investment banks and others, and tends to excessively reward a limited number of smart, lucky or in some cases dishonest executives and employees while harming or destroying the companies they manage and the savings and investments of a large percentage of our population. It did not promote economic prosperity for the common good. Instead, it has generated a financial system in which banks gamble with stockholders' and creditors' money and take unfair advantage of their customers. Teaser loan rates on adjustable rate mortgages given to home purchasers who make little or no down payment and high interest rate credit cards bleed the poor and the middle class families who over time find themselves unable to pay the outrageous interest and late fee charges on their excessive debt.

What appeared to be a recovery in the national economy and the labor market after 9/11/2001 was based on excess housing construction and related GDP growth encouraged by Congressmen and others who sought to promote home ownership for lower income families. It led to various irresponsible, deceptive and fraudulent mortgage related practices by our banks and investment banks, their executives and employees, use of excess leverage, speculators gaming the system and frauds by mortgage brokers, real estate agents, builders and non-qualified buyers.

Many of the manufacturing jobs lost over time had been high paying jobs that have been replaced by low paying retail, healthcare and fast food jobs. Many of the construction jobs created during the housing bubble were high paying jobs that were immediately eliminated after the housing bubble collapsed. Middle class salaries adjusted for inflation had been declining and following the Great Recession we find that median family net worth has declined precipitously. Home ownership even at lower prices has become less affordable for many Americans.

The soundness of our banking system, the fairness and stability of our securities industry, public and private debt problems, business growth, housing and infrastructure, welfare and entitlement issues are intertwined with job creation. The collapse of the housing and banking industries greatly intensified the jobs problem. The construction jobs created to build an excess number of houses and related local infrastructure have been lost, as have additional housing construction jobs lost temporarily while we reduce the excess housing inventory. The problem has been compounded as declining home prices and job losses have reduced the number of homeowners who can afford to remain in their homes or are willing to make payments on underwater mortgages, further exacerbating the number of unsold homes. The construction of apartments built to house families who have lost or delayed buying a home has created a significant number of good paying jobs, but construction of multiple family dwellings is less job intensive than home construction and has added to the excess of available housing units, which will slow a recovery in home prices.

The issues to resolve are gargantuan. Reduced employment in the housing and banking industries is both cyclical and structural. The banking industry is shedding jobs as banks are forced to reduce risk taking and the use of leverage as a result of the Dodd-Frank requirements that followed the losses they took from profligate lending. They have tightened their lending requirements and are making too few home loans. Housing problems are not going away unless we give major relief to homeowners or until millions of additional homes are foreclosed and sold. It can be argued that the people who bought homes they couldn't afford or who squandered their equity deserve their fate. However, The US economy and too many homeowners are suffering because of the wrongdoing of others. We must stop using outdated principles of free market capitalism as an excuse to prevent us from helping our suffering homeowners.

Many of the jobs lost to fabulous technological advances were domestic jobs while many of the jobs created by the technology companies, including those to manufacture the exceptional products they have created and some of the most skilled engineering positions, have gone to cheaper or more cooperative labor in the developing economies. It has created an unemployment crisis that we seem incapable of dealing with.

Fabulous computers using advanced software unimaginable twenty years ago acting as word processors have eliminated millions of jobs of workers, including typists and bookkeepers. For example, a legal secretary who 50 years ago was using what we thought to be a modern efficient electrical typewriter and using carbon paper and white-out to correct errors often had to retype an entire page or document. One busy attorney often needed two secretaries and night-time help to get his or her work done. Eventually we saved secretarial time by cutting and pasting Xeroxed originals. Today with a high speed word processor one legal secretary can handle the work of three or four lawyers. An automobile, tractor or airplane far superior to those built twenty years ago can be produced using automation and far fewer man-hours. Almost all industries have benefitted from labor saving technology. It should have greatly improved the lives of almost all of our families. It hasn't because instead of growing our economy we reduced employment.

The last 10 years have been extremely disappointing for the American economy. The amazing technology created in large part by American genius, which included the spawning of the information revolution, could and should have resulted in a spectacular rise in the GDP as occurred in the developing nations, including the BRIC countries. If we hadn't permitted our bankers to squander trillions of dollars of wealth and had used the opportunity to modernize our infrastructure rather than watch it decay we could have witnessed compounded GDP growth of 5% or more, which would have materially increased tax revenues for our Federal and state governments and reduced their debts. We must find a way to reverse the economic malaise and grow our economy.

We should not be fooled by the insignificant job growth that has resulted from the stimulus efforts promoted by the Obama Administration. During his first two years as President, when his party had control of both the House and the Senate, he did not focus on our major economic problems, jobs, housing and the soon-to-be unaffordable Medicare and Medicaid entitlements or even on Social Security funding, which is easy to fix.

President Obama missed the opportunity to materially stimulate construction spending by squandering a substantial portion of the $830 billion of stimulus spending in ways that did not promote the creation of jobs. His poor allocation of the stimulus funds led to his later proposals to reduce withholding taxes and increase welfare payments, which were further failed Keynesian attempts to stimulate the economy. Apparently his overriding goal was to please his base and create an appearance of an upturn in the economy in time for his reelection campaign.

Many of our consumers have lost a substantial portion of their net worth and have excessive debt they are seeking to reduce. As a result of years of extortionist labor demands and incompetent governance, many of our states have seen their current and prospective obligations rise as a percentage of their GDP and have been forced to restrain spending. Because of rising salaries, health care and retirement costs, most states were limiting infrastructure spending even before the Great Recession at a time when our aging and inadequate national transportation infrastructure could no longer adequately support the needs of our businesses and individuals. It is only a matter of time before some states, and in particular those governed by liberal Democrats who because of their pro union stance tend to exacerbate rather than attempt to deal with their employee compensation problems, will be unable to meet their obligations and will appeal to the federal government for revenue sharing or a bailout.

Many conservative free market economists have without justification criticized QE1, QE2 and QE3 from inception. The positive effect of the Fed's actions (the "Bernanke put") on stock and commodities prices have created a wealth effect that stimulated our economy and created jobs which helped the US to avoid a depression. However we must recognize some negative side effects of QE1, QE2 and QE3. Low risk interest income earned by IRAs and pension plan investments has been greatly reduced leaving our retirees with less spendable income and made many of them eligible for food stamps.

The Fed is so concerned about the fragile nature of our economic recovery, the weak housing market and bank solvency that it has adopted QE3 and committed to keeping interest rates low to help the US economy, banks and the housing market until 2014 or longer. It was done to encourage lending, since banks can rely on having cheap money available to them for years. Many argue that the Fed should not have made a long-term commitment or should reconsider such a policy whenever it appears that the economy is doing better than expected. In response to criticism of such a long-term commitment, some Fed members have spoken about the Fed's option to change its policy at any time if conditions improve. In other words, such members believe a promise is a promise until they change their mind. Rely on it at your peril.

Some economists believe that QE3 will not be effective because interest rates are already low and it is the equivalent of pushing on a string. Now the Fed is engaged in the questionable practices of buying high risk MBSes. The Fed's balance sheet has been weakened and by lowering short term interest rates to zero it has created a government bond bubble and limited its ability to promote further aid to the banks and stimulus to the economy. When the inevitable rise in interest rates occurs, it will generate a new wave of losses from investments in long-term bonds. The Fed's low interest rate policies have temporarily reduced the cost of carrying the surging national debt and masked future interest rate charges. A rise in interest rates on treasury securities unless offset by GDP growth is going to add materially to the federal deficit.

Many millions of Americans still lack good jobs. We continue to suffer from both cyclical and structural unemployment. Congress at the urging of President Obama extended the term of unemployment insurance to 99 weeks or beyond the point where it became a new welfare program.

Our financially stressed states with inadequate US government assistance are making only an inadequate effort to repair and improve our roads, bridges and tunnels. Our Congress and our voters are confused over the advisability of additional US government stimulus spending sought by President Obama for transportation infrastructure spending. Such needed spending will face major political hurdles because of the Fiscal Cliff and the more than $6 trillion dollars increase in the national debt to over $16 trillion during the Obama administration.

Most Americans are clueless as to how they and their children will be affected by the national debt. They know the US is a rich country which spends billions of dollars on all sorts of programs. Their lives are not being affected in any discernable way by the size of the debt. However when interest rates rise dramatically within the next few years the dollar will become subject to inflationary pressures that are going to impact them. Although the SNAP (food stamp) program is adjusted for inflation there is a lag time before the adjustment is made. Increased welfare costs are likely to further increase the federal deficit and lead to still higher rates of inflation.

If such inflationary spiral occurs then unless wages keep pace with inflation (which has not happened in recent years) the purchasing power of wage earners will decline and the disposable income spread between taxpayers and welfare beneficiaries will narrow. At such time conservatives will make a concerted effort to freeze or reduce welfare benefits. In other words unless we grow our economy our problems may soon resemble those faced by the southern European nations. Conservatives are correct in worrying that our economy faces potentially catastrophic dangers, but they are clueless as to the steps our government should take to avoid them. Liberal Democrats appear ready to accept unlimited debt to support excessive welfare programs and entitlements. They are hopeful that private industry will invest to stimulate growth, but their stimulus programs, Obamacare, Dodd-Frank and the American Taxpayer Relief Act of 2012 all discourage business investment.

By comparison, China, facing a slowdown, announced a $150 billion construction stimulus program in September 2012. China's new government to gain popularity is likely to further stimulate the Chinese economy. We have a much bigger economy than China. We need hundreds of billions of dollars of infrastructure spending as soon as possible. If we can find a way to fund our infrastructure needs, we will create hundreds of thousands of construction jobs almost immediately and jump-start the economy. It will generate significant additional demand in the auto and other consumer dependent industries leading to significant additional job growth. Job growth will help end the housing crisis and stimulate additional jobs in home construction and lead us into a strong cyclical upturn.

Although he from time to time expressed concern about housing problems and proposed worthless mortgage relief plans intending to help homeowners, President Obama has largely ignored the mortgage crisis. His first time home buyer's credit and the Dodd-Frank's provisions aimed at assisting home buyers by providing mortgage advice and limiting prepayment penalties are like putting a band aid on an a ruptured artery, virtually useless. Too many homeowners who have underwater mortgages will still lose their home and all mortgage payments and expenditures they made to improve it. Others will lose a substantial portion of the equity that grew over many years.

President Obama may feel that the Fed's low interest rate policies and purchase by investors and foreigners will eventually lead to a housing recovery. However, since all his speeches focused on getting reelected he apparently feels that voters are blaming our banks for the crisis and is letting the banks suffer one loss after another from the foreclosure mess. Talking about the mortgage crisis might have called attention to his egregious failure to help homeowners and interfered with his getting reelected. Instead, he made numerous empty speeches about his concern for the middle class. It may be that there were not enough affected homeowners who might have voted for him to matter. Governor Romney made only an inept attempt to focus on the failure of the Obama administration to help the middle class.

Arguments have surfaced that housing should not be considered a sound long term investment because of the maintenance requirements as a result of normal wear and tear. Such a position fails to take into account the fact that inflation and home improvements owners make while enjoying their homes should more than offset the decline from aging, and except for the decline caused by the housing bubble have historically left the owner with a materially appreciated investment over time.

Some of the potential home buyers are for a variety of reasons currently renting homes and apartments and waiting on the sidelines unconvinced of the inevitable effect of inflation over time on home prices and the expected long term benefits of home ownership. Renters do not enjoy the many social and financial benefits of home ownership and spend their money making other people rich. The housing bubble temporarily caused an excessive rise in housing prices, but if it had been prevented fewer houses would have been built and the price of housing would be higher than it is currently.

After long delays banks are now taking steps to foreclose an increased number of defaulted mortgages. Some of our investment vultures are organizing funds to invest billions of dollars in homes at very depressed foreclosure prices and to renovate the homes and put them up for rental and sale. They will profit from the failure of our government to help distressed homeowners and the continued incompetence of our bankers who can't figure out how to deal with the troubled mortgages in a way to reduce their losses. Prices are beginning to rise because of purchases by investors and foreigners, but it will do very little to help the homeowners with underwater mortgages or those whose equity built over a lifetime has all but disappeared.

Looking For Solutions

President Obama proposed to pay for what he calls temporary assistance for those down on their luck by taxing those he calls rich who already were paying a large portion of their income on federal and state taxes. Despite his demagoguery, more than half of the people he proposed to hit with tax increases are not rich. The American Taxpayer Relief Act of 2012 enacted by Congress immediately after going over the Fiscal Cliff, might reduce the federal deficit slightly in the short term, but will discourage economic growth. The tax increases will not raise enough revenue to prevent annual trillion dollar increases in the national debt, inevitably leading to Democratic liberals demanding further tax increases on the rich and the middle class, which if passed will likely result (as is happening in Europe) in a larger downturn in the economy.

As repeatedly stated herein, we must stop focusing on balancing the budget in the near term and find a way to grow the GDP at a faster rate than the rate of growth of our national debt. It is not the previous tax rates that were causing the federal and state revenue shortfalls but the lack of jobs. We must continue to promote the American policy of encouraging and rewarding effort. We must find a way to stimulate the economy to produce large numbers of quality jobs that will generate substantially higher tax revenues whether at current or revised tax rates.

If we create 10 million new jobs and U6 unemployment is reduced to an accurately counted 5 or 6% from the actual current rate of 15% or more, the current tax rates would produce sufficient revenues to reduce the annual federal deficit by hundreds of billions of dollars

We should consider adopting make-work programs of the type carried out during the Franklin Roosevelt administration to provide jobs during the Great Depression. One important difference is that today we have real needs for infrastructure transportation construction spending which would be revenue producing, as well as the need to improve schools and other public buildings.

There is an alternative way to finance many of our needed construction projects. We can seek investments in state construction projects from our cash rich businesses and wealthy individuals. It is time for people who have amassed great wealth to be encouraged to step up and invest in American transportation infrastructure projects to help jump-start the American economy.

We must also help homeowners. A large number of people feel that many buyers were complicit in the fraud and don't deserve assistance. Others believe that it is the nature of capitalism that you suffer losses if you make a bad investment. They don't care that the precipitous drop in home prices, which resulted in home owner losses, in large part have resulted from fraudulent or reckless acts of others and failed governmental regulation.

There are currently more than four million outstanding underwater mortgages whose principal amounts exceed the value of the home. There are millions of additional homes with minimal equity. Each foreclosure for the moment reduces by one the number of remaining underwater mortgages. However, the low prices of homes sold in foreclosure proceedings in recent years created further downward pressure on home prices that put additional mortgages underwater. The home price decline has abated in many parts of the country as foreign purchasers wishing to transfer a portion of their assets to the US and bargain hunters have been moving in to buy homes generally for cash. There has also been an increase in new home sales from very depressed levels, but it is insignificant in the total housing and jobs picture.

Many people who consider themselves free-market capitalists believe that homeowners should get no relief and that foreclosures should go forward even if ultimately 1/3 or 1/2 of homeowners lose their homes and prices fall another 10 or 15% or more before the market stabilizes. They believe that you create a moral hazard if you modify the mortgages of people who bought houses they couldn't afford or who refinanced their mortgages to excessive levels and are now in default. Permitting the bankers who received bonuses and capital gains of hundreds of millions of dollars by reporting fraudulent profits before the collapse and not bringing criminal or at least civil charges against them where appropriate to claw back the illegitimate profits is the real moral hazard growing out of the housing and banking bubbles. The bankers were responsible for the wrongdoing of the banks. Many of the suffering homeowners are innocent victims or were duped into purchasing homes they couldn't afford or into signing unfair mortgages.

THE OBAMA PRESIDENCY

President Obama did not possess the business knowledge or experience desirable for a person about to become President of the US during the Great Recession. His background better qualified him as a political activist. He previously had associated himself with other political activists who were outspoken critics of the US and free market capitalism. When he was elected in November of 2008 the US was in the midst of a financial crisis. He celebrated his victory and appointed qualified liberal economists and others who had assisted him in his successful campaign to help him deal with economic issues.

The President of the US by reason of his position is the most powerful man in the world. President Obama is not using that power to promote American greatness. Most importantly President Obama has failed to lead our economy back to prosperity. He inherited an economic crisis, but he and his advisers had never prior to his reelection campaign indicated an understanding of the immensity of the problems. He came to office during the Great Recession that had threatened to cause our economy to spiral downward into a deep depression until TARP was adopted under President George W. Bush and QE 1 was adopted by the Fed, both of which took place before President Obama took office. Those actions stabilized the banking system. After he won the election in November 2008, he prepared for his inaugural ball when he should have been focusing on dealing with the declining economy that had been mostly ignored but rapidly deteriorating for many months during the 2008 election campaign.

President Obama got elected making moving campaign speeches offering hope and change for the future. After being elected, he and the Democratic controlled Congress failed to develop a comprehensive plan to create jobs needed to generate a substantial recovery from the Great Recession. As President he has exhibited brilliant oratory skills with the aid of a teleprompter but his stimulus programs have squandered trillions of dollars and done very little to stimulate the creation of new jobs, end the housing crisis or lead our country out of the Great Recession.

Looking back, we see that G.W. Bush up against a hostile Congress and critical Democratic campaign for the presidency managed to propose and get Congress to adopt TARP to avoid a total collapse of the economy and the auto industry during the final six months of has administration. The inaction by Congress exposed a major flaw in the American political system. Our Congress is virtually shut down during the period of at least six months preceding a presidential election (and to a lesser extent every two years) as both parties vie to gain the presidency and both houses of Congress. The delay in dealing with the Great Recession before and immediately after the election had a similar effect as withholding antibiotics from a patient with a serious infection permitting it to get much worse. While our leaders delayed, the economy spiraled downward.

President Obama and his advisers were apparently unaware of the extent of the problem when he took office. When President Obama realized that the US economy was in a tailspin, to his credit and over conservative Republican objections he recognized the need to stimulate the economy. However, he followed bad economic advice and his own personal preferences.

President Obama's advisers put together an inadequate, badly conceived and politically motivated stimulus package passed by a Democratic controlled Congress on February 23, 2009. President Obama and his Keynesian economic advisors apparently felt that the stimulus package would be effective because of its size no matter how the funds were spent.

The Obama administration expected that unemployment would quickly decline and the economy would recover as in past downturns. It is apparent that President Obama and his advisors did not fully comprehend the extent of the losses our banks, homeowners, investors, credit card users and retirees had incurred and the effect it would have on jobs, the housing market and overall consumer spending.

A large portion of his stimulus program was spent giving almost all taxpayers a $500 gift intended to be a Keynesian stimulus but which proved ineffective because, as should have been anticipated, many people used it to reduce debt or purchase products manufactured overseas. He devoted a large portion of the remaining stimulus funds on politically motivated projects. The Democrats should have known better and adjusted their stimulus program to create American jobs that would have increased taxable income and reduced the number of welfare recipients. For example, the Obama stimulus plan included large sums to guaranty loans to entities involved in the development of solar power and other alternative energy projects that he thought would become the future energy producers but which hired few employees.

The problem with the loan guarantees for companies with unproven technology and little more than a fancy power point presentation is that political leaders and their advisors are rarely good at selecting entities to fund that will be successful. The US government was taking most of the risk and the start-up entities and their highly paid executives would, if successful, have kept most of the profits. Billions of dollars of funding went down the drain when the companies failed. If he wanted to fund research he could have given grants to universities for such purpose, which probably would have resulted in the development of better products at a small fraction of the cost.

His advisers who were preoccupied with concerns of global warming obstructed the revolution that was taking place in producing energy from shale that despite his interference has been the most important economic development to take place and largest producer of jobs during his administration.

His words and actions have made it clear that he favors excessive government control of our lives over a regulated free market economy that promotes and rewards individual effort and business accomplishments.

Too small a portion of the stimulus package was made available for shovel ready construction and other domestic job creating projects. The money his plan gave to the states to shore up their finances barely scratched the surface of the problem and has been offset by the added Medicaid burdens Obamacare will place upon the states.

To get reelected after his initial stimulus program failed the president sought other ways to stimulate the economy. He convinced Republicans to extend unemployment benefits to a total of 99 weeks, to extend all of the Bush income tax reductions and to adopt withholding tax reductions and then extend them for an additional year. By doing so he gave additional money to consumers, but did not add a significant number of taxpaying jobs. The Fiscal Cliff did not occur by accident. President Obama timed the extensions of the Bush tax cuts and arranged for other tax increases and spending reductions to be effective after the election, which led to the Fiscal Cliff. Hopefully Congress will learn from the Fiscal Cliff that they shouldn't pass tax laws with sunset provisions.

President Obama promoted the SNAP (food stamp) program that added over 15 million additional beneficiaries. Under the guise of helping "folks" who are down on their luck or unfortunate he is transforming America from the land of opportunity where individual effort led to one's success to a run-of-the-mill socialist country where one-half of the population have few if any job opportunities to pursue the American dream and whether they want to or not live off the efforts of the other half.

Working people live a better life. They contribute more to society, including paying income tax and have much higher self-esteem than those living off public handouts. Socialism has generally failed to improve living standards. It takes wealth from those who earned it and dissipates it by giving it away while discouraging the recipients from finding ways to be productive. Confiscating wealth from the rich, if adopted, is likely to have only a limited short-term effect, if any, on reducing the US government deficit and will prove disastrous to our economy in the long run.

President Obama takes credit for saving the auto industry and misleadingly claimed throughout the election campaign that Governor Romney would have let GM and Chrysler go out of business because private funding was not available. Such claim was nonsensical but many voters bought it. President Obama did recognize the importance of saving the auto industry (as did almost all Americans, including President George W Bush who used TARP money to keep the industry operating), but the manner in which he chose to do so was disgraceful. Governor Romney or almost any other president would have saved the auto industry (as we have repeatedly saved airlines) in a more conventional manner, which would have better served it and its employees in the long term.

President Obama disregarded long-recognized contract laws and bankruptcy principles by insisting that secured creditors give up their right to share in the reorganized auto companies while protecting the unsecured claims of the union pension plans. This leaves GM and Chrysler less competitive than other manufacturers because it increases the cost of each car and restricts the type of cars they can design and sell profitably. He also gave stock ownership to the United Auto Workers Union, an unsecured creditor and an Obama supporter (and not the secured creditors who under contract were entitled to it). The US government could have financed the restructuring of the auto industry with TARP type loans in ordinary bankruptcy proceedings.

While saving GM, the approach he supported eliminated important brands such as Pontiac, Saturn and Hummer and closed about half of the dealerships, eliminating many hundreds of thousands of jobs. This in turn eliminated many additional jobs at our auto suppliers.

It is unlikely that an auto company owned in substantial part by its union and saddled with high pension obligations will over time be able to compete competitively. Because the secured creditors received less than they were entitled, it is going to be difficult for GM and Chrysler to borrow money in the future except from the US government. President Obama's appointees have steered GM into producing the Volt, a battery propelled car, which pleases environmentalists but misread consumer preferences.

President Obama has an incomplete record as the most important player in the game of macroeconomics. He remains committed to failed Keynesian stimulus programs of a type that had been effective in the 20th Century. He stubbornly relies on stimulus efforts which are not working under current economic conditions. They have added $6 trillion to the national debt, but have not helped millions of Americans, many of whom were members of the middle class who have lost their jobs or a substantial portion of their wealth or whose home mortgages are upside down or in foreclosure.

Instead of paying attention to job creation and the failures of his stimulus plan he concentrated his efforts on passing and promoting Obamacare and the Dodd-Frank banking law each of which have impeded rather than promoted the recovery of the economy.

Perpetuating American greatness has become more difficult as a result of (i) the European downturn caused in part by the monetary crisis and the austerity programs forced upon the debt burdened Southern European nations, (ii) the explosion of debt at all levels of government in the US and (iii) the risk of a slowdown from China and the developing nations. Furthermore, the failure to stimulate the US economy has contributed to the risk of a worldwide slowdown.

The failure of President Obama to promote a sound recovery has squandered years of potential growth in our economy that would have slowed the growing federal and state debts. While the growth in the US economy and government revenues have stagnated, the looming entitlement crisis is getting closer as more people reach retirement age, medical costs rise as new treatments and procedures become available and our population lives longer.

Except to the extent that Medicare funding was reduced under Obamacare, which will lead to reduced benefits, President Obama is ignoring the coming threat to our economy from mushrooming entitlements that will need to be modified to be sustainable. He stonewalled demands by Republicans that entitlements be dealt with as part of the negotiations relating to the resolution of the Fiscal Cliff. The failure to adequately grow the GDP is going to make it more difficult to deal with entitlement issues.

President Obama does not appear to be paying enough attention to the potential risks of terrorism on our shores that could at any moment disrupt our lives and the economic recovery. The excessive length of time it took to restore power generation that prolonged the disruption in gasoline distribution after hurricane Sandy is indicative of a lack of preparedness to deal with problems that could arise at any time as a result of a terrorist act.

Rather than putting politics aside and focusing on job creation and ending the housing crisis President Obama chose to and continues to blame all of our economic problems on past failures of President George W. Bush and the current policies of Republicans for being obstructionists and refusing to support his failed policies.

President Obama blames the banking and housing bubbles on failed deregulation policies favored by Republicans years ago while he ignores the fact that the leftist social objectives advocated principally by Democrats were in large part to blame for promoting outrageously irresponsible no documentation or no down payment mortgage loans made by the banks and purchased by FNMA and Freddie Mac. Those purchases in turn led to the securitization of high-risk mortgages and to the banking and housing bubbles that collapsed causing the Great Recession. Democrats like Barney Frank accept none of the blame for the Great Recession but they pushed insatiably for many years for banks to give mortgage financing and issue credit cards to borrowers who were not credit worthy prior to and during the presidency of George W. Bush.

In the mid to late 1990s, President Obama represented claimants in a class action against Citi Bank claiming discriminatory lending practices in the Chicago area, which was settled and resulted in Citi Bank giving mortgages to about 350 of the claimants. It has been reported that a high percentage of the borrowers have defaulted on the mortgages and many of them have gone bankrupt since receiving the mortgage financing. President Obama has blamed bad loans as a source of the housing collapse. President Obama and other ultra-liberal Democrats shared the responsibility for promoting loans to borrowers who couldn't afford to pay them.

Obamacare passed with a concentrated effort while the Democrats controlled both the presidency and both houses of Congress, is almost certain to develop into the largest of our entitlement programs. By expanding health care coverage for the uninsured, changing the way that insurance is offered and mandating insurance coverage in a law which no-one could understand the consequences of, they added what will turn out to be trillions of dollars to future health care entitlement costs while using gimmicks to enable them to fraudulently claim that they were reducing health care costs. In the short time since it has passed, the Congressional Budget Office has changed its evaluation of the effect of Obamacare on the deficit from its having a positive effect to its adding $1.75 trillion to the deficit. It was the wrong bill for America in 2009. It made the economic problems much worse by creating uncertainty for businesses trying to recover from the Great Recession.

The finding of the Supreme Court that a part of Obamacare is constitutional as a tax highlights the fact that President Obama raised taxes (or if you prefer, created penalties) at the height of the Great Recession, a clear no-no for job creation. For political reasons, the Democrats deferred the Obamacare tax increases until after the 2012 election.

President Obama has not championed and even apologizes for our government's past history of attempting to promote individual rights and freedom throughout the world. He has failed to take the lead in assisting in the formation of American styled democracies in the countries affected by the Arab Spring. He has failed to support friendly governments that have been overthrown and are being replaced by governments that although they call themselves democracies, are in large part dominated by leaders with terrorist backgrounds.

We are giving substantial financing and military aid to the new governments. However, unless we take a more active role, there is a serious risk that terrorist organizations with the aid of Iran and other nations antagonistic toward the US gain control of some of the newly formed and fragile democracies.

The President takes credit for the killing of Osama Bin Laden, but to get reelected he hid from the American people the fact that Al Qaeda and other terrorist organizations are gaining power in many parts of the world and were responsible for the murder of our ambassador and others in Libya.

No one wants to see our military personnel killed and maimed fighting to install or protect corrupt democracies that deny civil rights to their people, but we must be prepared to fight to insure that control of these countries does not pass to terrorist organizations seeking to destroy the US and our allies.

President Obama has for political reasons hastened to bring our troops home from Iraq and Afghanistan despite the risk that he is converting hard earned victories into defeats. He is further weakening our military strength by reducing the size of our armed forces and military spending. He doesn't recognize the importance of our military superiority and our support for people seeking freedom from tyranny to the war against terrorism and the preservation of American greatness.

President Obama cites the cost of the Iraq and Afghanistan wars as a major cause of our government deficits. Nothing could be farther from the truth. For example the production ramp-up for World War II was job intensive, greatly expanded our economy and played a vital role in helping our economy escape from the Great Depression.

We should remember that we profited from the First Gulf War because Saudi Arabia reimbursed the US for much of the cost of the First Gulf War and that we failed to obtain any direct reimbursement for the later wars. Our businesses should be benefiting from the rebuilding of the Iraq economy after the war, but the premature removal of our troops and the failure of our president to take a leadership role may be jeopardizing such participation.

The Iraq and Afghanistan wars increased the revenues of our defense industries, which created jobs and tax revenues (and had the added benefit of strengthening our defensive capabilities which are seriously declining under President Obama), and helped mask the structural employment problem accelerating after the turn of the century.

President Obama will gladly accept the pending required reductions in military spending included in the Fiscal Cliff which the foolish Republican leadership insisted on to force him to reduce future government spending. He nonsensically claims he will use the savings from the Iraq and Afghan wars to finance education expenditures.

What President Obama fails to understand is that reducing military expenditures and reducing the size of the military is negatively impacting our economy, and as defense workers get laid off the multiplier effect will lead to further job losses. What his rapid troop reduction is doing is adding many of our returning veterans to the unemployment rolls. His pleas to business (joined in by well-intentioned groups) that we find jobs for returning veterans will help returning veterans who deserve employment. However, doing so will not add many new jobs but take jobs away from high school and college graduates and others among the unemployed seeking jobs.

President Obama is playing Russian roulette with our economy. He began with Democratic control of Congress and had his own agenda. The Democrats raced to adopt Obamacare and the Dodd-Frank legislation before they were understood or debated to eliminate glaring errors some of which are slowly being corrected.

President Obama claims the Republicans have refused to compromise, but from the time he took office to the end of his first term he has conducted the presidency his way and with no intention to compromise. He seemed content during the presidential campaign claiming that the economy was getting better (based on small job growth and minor increases in the GDP) and waiting until after the election to deal with the potential catastrophe that awaited the next president.

President Obama told voters during the election campaign that a recovery was underway. He cited the meager growth in the GDP resulting from tax reductions that were due to end and on a misleading reduction in headline unemployment. He disregarded the fact that the meager job increases pall when compared to job growth in the recovery periods which followed previous recessions.

He talked during the campaign about raising taxes a little bit more on millionaires and billionaires to finance his planned growth in spending but he really meant raising taxes on families earning more than $250,000. He ignored the fact that he had already created additional income taxes on these families as part of the Obamacare legislation. He knew that such families, whom he called rich are, not rich, but middle class if they live in most large cities, and are having difficulty paying their bills. In order to obtain passage of the American Taxpayer Relief Act of 2012 he limited his demand for a tax rate increase to individuals earning over $400,000 and families earning over $450,000 but managed to increase income taxes on families earning over $300,000 by phasing out some of their deductions.

He knew that the tax increases included in the American Taxpayer Relief Act of 2012 will not raise enough revenue to materially reduce the Federal deficit and will discourage job creation. If such tax increases lead to job layoffs or reduce capital spending or hiring, they might even increase the size of the deficit.

As we approached the edge of the Fiscal Cliff and the Congressional Budget Office (CBO) stated inaction would cause a serious downturn in the economy in 2013 many businessmen, investors and economists became alarmed about the possibility of Congressional gridlock. President Obama rather than make a serious attempt to negotiate with the Republicans took his proposed resolution of the Fiscal Cliff to the voters who elected him. He used the expiring Bush tax cuts on low-income people as a club to force the Republicans into submission to gain passage of the tax increases he wanted.

President Obama's policies throughout his Presidency have frightened businessmen who have for many months been delaying hiring and capital expenditures or laying off workers in anticipation of the Fiscal Cliff, the costs of Obamacare, problems caused by Dodd-Frank, and concerns about a slowdown in the economy. The tax changes that have been adopted are not likely to ease such concerns.

President Obama claims he is the champion of the middle class. During the election campaign he talked about growing the economy from the middle out or the bottom up (whatever those words may mean). Paradoxically, the middle class is the group that has endured the greatest suffering under President Obama's failed policies.

President Obama's proposal to hire 100,000 math and science teachers was made for political purposes. Although teaching jobs represent good paying jobs which would be beneficial to our economy and to the education process it is a meaningless number compared to the total number of jobs we need. In any event, we couldn't find and place anywhere near that number of competent teachers within a year or two to teach students who aren't prepared to learn in our inadequate schools. Politicians for years have sought to improve education. We spend large amounts with poor results. Grade school education is provided and paid for at the state and local level. We must first figure out a way enable parents to put their children in schools that give teachers a better teaching environment and improve the opportunity for students to learn. We must also encourage parents to use the teaching tools available on television, at libraries and on the Internet to make learning enjoyable and to help their children learn at home. Despite Governor Romney's ill-advised attack on the US government funding of Big Bird (a highly profitable super star performer for many years), our children obviously need more than Big Bird and his companions to further their education. Keeping middle class families in their homes will greatly benefit education.

Governor Romney faced a political dilemma. A large group from the religious right of the conservative Republican base whose votes he needed, have in recent years promoted a rising role of religion in political thought that has produced candidates who emphasize the right-to-life and related issues. Certain of them gain national publicity by claiming to be the true conservative candidate, and their campaigns turned moderates, liberals and women away from the Republican party and made it much more difficult for the Republican nominee to defeat the President.

They gave the Obama administration and the liberal press almost daily opportunities to distract from the President's economic and military failures by changing the campaign issues from jobs, housing and rising threats of terrorism to deliberately sensationalized events relating to a broad range of civil rights matters.

President Obama campaigned for reelection from the day he took office. During the course of the reelection campaign he created trumped up confrontations with Republicans and then flew to a college campus or a business location in a swing state to hold a press conference trumpeted by the liberal press to make a populous speech filled with demagoguery designed to make it look like he cares and the Republican's don't care about the civil rights of women, minorities or immigrants. The President's statements were all politically motivated to garner votes from blacks, Hispanics, gays, women and young people and to cause confrontations with Conservative Republicans. He generated fear among women that the religious right through its influence in the Republican party would seek to deprive women of birth control and abortion rights that are long since settled and would not have been at risk if Governor Romney won the presidential election. The exit polls showed that a large percentage of the people who voted for President Obama focused solely on such issues and paid little attention to his claims that the economy was improving.

President Obama misled the voters as to the state of the US economy. He admitted his economic failures and blamed them on the Great Recession inherited from George W. Bush. He cited meager job and GDP growth in the last two years as proof that the economy is headed in the right direction. He didn't talk about his failed stimulus, jobs created by the Fed and our international companies dealing with the BRIC countries or the Fiscal Cliff. Unfortunately it's easy to mislead the American voter. Instead of getting his wealthiest supporters to invest in jump starting the US economy he used some of them who do not have substantial income subject to ordinary tax rates to support his worthless plan to tax the people he calls rich a little bit more. His statements about the Fiscal Cliff make it clear that he is preparing to blame the Republicans for the anticipated weakness in the US economy in the next two years before the mid-term elections.

President Obama raised taxes on the wrong group of taxpayers. He should have sought to close the tax loopholes that allow the truly high-income taxpayers who earn their income as a carried interest and pay low capital gains tax rates. However, many of the hedge fund and private equity managers benefitting from such low tax rates are major contributors to politicians of both parties and politicians give favored tax treatment to their supporters.

The President has won the election, but he faces a very challenging economic situation. He will have the opportunity to become one of the great American presidents. However, if he fails to take steps to greatly improve job creation he is likely to be remembered for creating runaway inflation or like Herbert Hoover as the president who led us into a horrible depression. His past actions as president that included ramming through Obamacare and Dodd-Frank are negatively impacting economic growth. President Obama is treating his reelection as an affirmation of Obamacare and Dodd-Frank even though most of the voters didn't even think about them. At the very least he should be looking for ways to modify and improve each of them. The unbecoming manner in which he and his supporters conducted his campaign and handled the Fiscal Cliff will not be forgotten by the Republican leadership and is likely to make his task of dealing with the economy more difficult.

President Obama is serving in his second term. His first term performance leaves many unfulfilled promises and relies on blaming former president Bush and the Republicans for his failures. It seems inevitable that even if the Republicans do not give in to all of his demands, if the country goes back into recession or if we have runaway inflation, President Obama will be held responsible.

THE FUTURE OF THE US ECONOMY

It is unclear whether the Great Recession has come to an end or we are witnessing a pause in the downturn that will lead us into a double dip recession or a depression.

Reports that the US economy is still growing slowly overlook the fact that it is not likely to be sustainable because it was being supported by tax reductions that are being reduced under the new tax law. Unless we find a way to avoid job losses that may result and to stimulate job growth our national debt will continue to mushroom. The world economy, particularly Europe needs a stable and growing US economy for support.

The government stimulus should have been better designed to create wealth and jobs. Welfare spending may put food on the table but after it is eaten it is gone. The building of improved roads, bridges, tunnels, airports and even government buildings creates assets of lasting value that benefit our states, cities, businesses and individuals and make our economy more efficient. Construction projects are labor intensive, creating large numbers of domestic jobs at salary levels which generate substantial income taxes for our federal and state governments promote consumer spending, auto sales, home purchases, and create demand for raw materials and equipment.

The argument that the construction jobs end when the project is completed is without merit. We have more than a 10-year backlog of needed construction projects. It is difficult to assess how much our economy benefitted in recent years from the construction spending that followed the hurricanes, tornedos, floods and other natural disasters. Funding that was supplied by FEMA, state contingency reserves and private insurance recoveries and personal savings, played a significant role in the nascent recovery from the Great Recession and was probably more effective than the much larger Obama stimulus plan.

Preoccupation with the Fiscal Cliff and debt and entitlement issues has distracted the president and Congress from dealing with job creation. Paradoxically, the catastrophic losses caused by hurricane Sandy will over time help to grow the US economy. After the initial shock and a downturn caused by business interruptions and closings, a large number of jobs will be generated in connection with the cleanup, repair and replacement efforts, which will be financed in large part by FEMA funding and insurance proceeds.

The national debt is heading toward dangerous levels unless the GDP begins to grow at an accelerated rate. On the positive side, the slowly expanding economy coupled with strict cost controls (including layoffs or limited hiring) and growth in the developing countries has led to increased business profits and a stock market recovery. The wealth effect supported by QE1, QE2 and QE3 has supported high-end retail spending. However, economic growth has been constrained because capital spending by business has been discouraged by the adoption of Obamacare, Dodd-Frank and the failed stimulus, the Fiscal Cliff, and the problems in Europe. The cyclical recovery is anemic and not the type of recovery expected after a significant downturn and substantial stimulus spending.

Our federal and state governments collect a substantial portion of their revenues from earned income. It is the shortage of good paying jobs and not the current tax rates that are causing large revenue shortfalls. President Obama talks of spending (which he calls investing to make it sound more acceptable whether or not it produces an asset of lasting value) on a broad variety of items such as education, alternative energy and infrastructure. However, his blunderbuss politically oriented approach squandered much of his previous stimulus funding.

Our political system is both broken and gridlocked. Leftist leaning liberals and rightist conservatives criticize each other and promote programs that will likely exacerbate rather than alleviate our economic problems. Both political parties seemed more concerned with misleading the voters to try to win the 2012 elections than in taking actions to deal with the approaching Fiscal Cliff, create job opportunities for all Americans and resolve the banking, housing and entitlement crises. Our politicians and economists assert that they know the legislative route to create jobs and economic prosperity and reduce the national debt. Unfortunately, most of their proposals would be of little or no help and might be counter-productive and hurt the nascent recovery.

Congress acts like a sailing ship dead in the water with no wind except when its members make politically motivated speeches. Members of both parties propose tax changes that might be marginally beneficial or detrimental. Some Republicans, including the leadership in the House of Representatives, are paranoid about the growing national debt. They know that our federal government can print money if necessary to pay its debts and inflate its way out of the problem, but they also worry about inflation. They do not seem to understand that deflation, which Mr. Bernanke feared, is much worse than the mild inflation he is promoting. Inflation should over time lead to an increase in home values. The danger is that if inflation gets out of control it will lead to an interest rate spiral and raise the burden of the national debt.

A majority of Americans do not understand the importance of the national debt and have not even considered the possibility of or potential effect of inflation. They believe that President Obama's efforts to run the country with the advice of his advisors are being obstructed by Republicans who care only about the rich. Many of them have given up looking for a good job to attain upward mobility and have accepted the status quo of living with a low paying or part time job and a financial safety net.

Our politicians and economists talk about jobs being an important concern. They know that our economy is not sustainable without job growth. They argue over what should be done to encourage job creation. None of the proposals except President Obama's transportation infrastructure construction spending proposals or Governor Romney's proposals to increase military spending and to promote energy independence, whether advocated by supply siders, Keynesians, budget balancers, socialists, conservatives or others, are likely to significantly accelerate the economy or create needed job growth.

Some people argue that government spending does not create jobs. That is not true. Needed spending by government on transportation infrastructure construction will create jobs. President Obama's transportation infrastructure spending proposals, passed by Congress in 2012, were a baby step in the right direction but they pale when compared to the wasteful spending included in his stimulus plan. He now proposes an Infrastructure Bank to support transportation infrastructure construction. Unfortunately, he has expended his political capital on Obamacare, Dodd-Frank, and his failed stimulus program and can't get Congress to approve a large enough increase in transportation infrastructure construction spending to create jobs. Unless we find an alternative way to finance infrastructure construction spending our federal government and the states are not likely to significantly increase and might even reduce such spending.

The failure of the US economy to rebound significantly and the unacceptably high levels of unemployment have raised a question few people want to consider, namely, is American democracy the best form of government? While China and other developing countries rapidly expand their economies and build new 21st Century cities for a million or more people the growth in our major cities comes mostly from foreign investors looking for a safe haven for some of their capital. Too many of our country's workers remain unemployed, underemployed or undercompensated. Our entitlements are in jeopardy of becoming unaffordable, our housing market remains in shambles and our transportation infrastructure and many of our schools and public buildings are in a state of decline.

Congressional inaction has been further complicated by the steep rise in the national debt under President Obama, which resulted in large part from the failure of his stimulus programs. Conservative Republicans for their own political purposes blame the government deficits in recent years on spending increases during both the Obama and George W. Bush administrations without distinguishing spending to create needed jobs and wealth creating expenditures from wasteful spending, leftist oriented welfare expenditures to temporarily (or indefinitely) relieve suffering and buy votes or pork expenditures to reward friends. Democrats criticize President George W. Bush's added spending to support the Iraq and Afghan wars without recognizing that military spending (an unplanned Keynesian stimulus which works) promotes job growth in the defense industry and stimulates the economy.

Many conservative Republicans claim that we can reduce the deficit by austerity measures in the form of a substantial reduction of government spending. Since macroeconomics is often counterintuitive, they might believe austerity will reduce the deficit or sound like responsible action and is appealing to many voters who are reducing their personal spending to reduce their debt. They may also have deluded themselves into thinking that reduced government spending accompanied by reduced corporate tax rates will lead to a substantial increase in private investment, which will create large numbers of jobs and a sustainable recovery.

To the contrary reduced US government spending is likely to lead to increased layoffs as corporations attempt to maintain short-term profits. The disastrous downturns in the economies of Greece and Spain (even though they have been given debt relief) and the European slowdown have made it clear that austerity measures will grow unemployment and increase, not decrease the deficit. Such an approach would likely result in a deep recession or a depression, a much larger federal deficit, Greek and Italian type interest rates and ultimately lead to printing dollars (which the Greek and Italian governments cannot do) to pay much higher rates of interest on our soaring national debt and lead to much higher rates of inflation.

Republicans are justified in objecting to reckless government expansion of entitlements without regard to cost. They have made an important start in introducing discussion of a plan to deal with long-term entitlements such as Social Security and Medicare and have rejected Obamacare. However, their demand for spending cuts as a pre-condition to approve routine type government actions such as raising the national debt limit or extending the reduced interest rate on student loans is interfering with the normal functioning of our government. Such silly positions weaken their arguments for fiscal responsibility and detract from the important failures of the Obama administration.

Governor Romney proposed corporate and individual tax reductions to be accompanied by offsetting reductions in tax credits and deductions and government spending to spur investment. Although he said he would not lower the taxes paid by high income taxpayers or raise taxes on the middle class, he gave President Obama the opportunity to argue that Governor Romney was going to have to raise taxes on the middle class to reduce the taxes on the wealthy. Governor Romney tried to clarify his tax proposals by promising that they would be passed only with bipartisan support and would not be adopted until it was clearly established that they would not harm the middle class in any manner. His supply side approach would have gotten bogged down in Congress and was not likely to be passed even if he had been elected President. It was an ill-advised proposal. It was not likely to promote business expansion or job creation unless his other spending proposals or other actions were taken to first jump-start growth in the economy.

Furthermore, to the extent that the reductions in government spending he was advocating represented austerity measures rather than a reduction in certain wasteful spending proposed by President Obama they would have been counterproductive. This is the wrong time in the recovery to cut spending. It is highly unlikely that we can curtail the deficit or the national debt without creating large numbers of jobs, which will generate substantial tax revenue, and at the same time reduce welfare expenditures for unemployment insurance, Medicaid, negative income taxes and food stamps. Said another way, we must get some of the welfare recipients out of the wagon and arrange for them to join the workforce and help pull the wagon. The wagon will be easier to pull when it gets lighter.

Our economy remains interdependent with the continued growth of the developing countries and economic stability in

Europe. The Southern European nations face many of the same problems we face in the US. Like our states they cannot print money. The housing and banking collapse in parts of Europe is contributing to the inability of some of Europe's governments to pay their debts. They do not have a central government to come to the aid of their banks with a program like TARP, but with fits and starts they are trying to solve that problem through a central monetary authority. They have an immense entitlement problem that they have tried to fix for years with very limited success while causing very high and rising unemployment. Unfortunately the austerity measures being forced on the Southern European nations by Germany and other Northern European nations as a condition of providing financial support for their bonds is deepening the recessions and causing skyrocketing unemployment in Southern European nations.

The European decline has slowed growth in the US economy and in the BRIC nations. If not abated it may send the world economy into recession. President Obama has tried to avoid getting involved with Europe's financial problems, but our recovery is clearly being impacted by the current downturn in Europe. Many of our business entities export products to European customers or sell products through subsidiaries in the European markets. On the other hand China is again stimulating its economy that may lead to an improvement in both the European and our economy. The world economy will benefit if we work in tandem with China.

JOBS, WAGES AND PROSPERITY

During The Great Recession the rapid decline in housing and securities prices and federal and state tax revenues and fees resulted in accelerated job losses, business failures and reduced consumer and public spending. The jobs problem reached crisis proportions as the US economy contracted sharply and cyclical unemployment added to already existing and growing structural unemployment. Millions of additional workers were laid off or not replaced upon retirement. The Great Recession accelerated the looming insolvency of many of our states, cities and municipalities resulting in work force reductions in the public sector, which had been a bastion of job security in prior downturns.

It could have been much worse. The collapse of our banks and of the housing market that wiped out a significant portion of our country's total net-worth caused the Great Recession. The problem became worse as monetary liquidity disappeared and a declining GDP led to further job losses, which could have led our economy into a depression. The main reasons our economy stabilized and did not continue downward into a depression spiral are (i) TARP loans stabilized the banking industry, (ii) jobs have been maintained or created by our strong profitable international businesses which are supplying products and services, food and commodities, to the developing economies, (iii) jobs have been created by wireless communication companies and newly formed and growing small businesses including Internet based entities and companies in other high tech industries, (iv) the Fed's adoption of QE1, QE2 and QE3 and then Operation Twist, which further strengthened our banks, and reduced mortgage rates and interest rates on bonds which in turn induced a recovery in stock market prices leading to strong high end consumer spending, and (v) to a lesser extent, from the limited support the economy received from the failed Obama February 2009 stimulus plan.

We watch on the first Friday of each month as CNBC, Bloomberg, Fox and other financial networks predict and then report and analyze in detail the report delivered by the Department of Labor (DOL) on changes in non-farm and government payrolls, the rate of unemployment and other job related information such as the number of hours worked and hourly wages of the prior month and revised information of recent months. This report, like most governmental reports, is highly flawed. For example, during September 2012 the DOL reported a large decline in unemployment because more than 300,000 people stopped looking for work and dropped out of the work force. Because they gave up looking for work, they were no longer counted as unemployed by the DOL in its top line unemployment number. The financial press should have been in an uproar over this misleading number but instead they cheered for the top line unemployment number to promote rising stock prices and the president's reelection.

We will never know how many of those people who we counted as unemployed and were collecting unemployment insurance benefits until their benefits ran out would have retired. Some of them were probably collecting while spending their time fishing, playing golf or working at home or on a job for an unreported cash payment. Many withdrew from the work force as soon as their benefits ran out. Extending unemployment insurance for seniors who would have retired had the effect of temporarily increasing the number of people claiming to be unemployed. When their benefits ran out and they retired and dropped out of the workforce, top line unemployment declined. However, many of them, including some of the seniors whose wealth was decimated by the Great Recession, would have looked for and taken a job if they thought one was available. Now that unemployment benefits have been extended again for 99 weeks we can expect a larger number of people to claim they are looking for work.

The DOL does a poor job of adjusting for seasonality and weather and makes certain other questionable arbitrary adjustments. As a result the definition used to calculate the number and percentage of unemployed makes the reported headline numbers misleading. However, it gives the financial reporters fodder for an exciting discussion and they make the headline number sound very important. Total unemployment of 23 million or about 15%, which counts the underemployed and discouraged workers, is reported under measure U6 in the same monthly report. Although the reporters treat the U6 unemployment number as if it is less important, it is far more relevant when evaluating the state of the economy than the headline number.

The October job's report showed a drop in headline unemployment below 8% based on some highly suspect numbers (like a large increase in the number of government jobs), but overall it was a disappointing report. The report became a heavily discussed campaign issue with President Obama and the liberal press claiming the economy is moving in the right direction while disregarding the more important total unemployment level including the underemployed and discouraged workers that remained at around 23 million people.

Many of the jobs created in the past two years are part time or low-paying dead-end jobs. Obamacare is encouraging small employers to offer part time work to limit health care costs. The simple fact remains that people who have lost their job and high school, college and even graduate students are having a difficult time finding (and many have given up looking for) what they consider to be worthwhile jobs with good pay. In many depressed areas across the country the man on the street will tell you that unemployment, particularly youth unemployment, remains rampant. A large percentage of our population is living on an assortment of expanded welfare payments to meet their needs.

We hear from employers about current job openings that cannot be filled because workers are unavailable where the demand exists or have the wrong skills. Many employers offering positions starting at approximately $40,000 per year are unable to fill them. There is an obvious unwillingness of welfare recipients to accept such positions and reduce their benefits. They would rather work part time or off the books. We must constantly review the disincentives to accepting work.

We hear a lot of talk of spending for education to teach the unemployed needed job specific skills. Our grade and high schools should provide all students with the opportunity to obtain basic math, reading, writing, and computer skills and should offer a variety of trade skills of the types needed by businesses in the immediate area for students to elect to pursue. We should be training students and arranging on-the-job training as apprentices in fields such as auto mechanics, bricklaying, plumbing, carpentering and upholstering.

In the high tech world in which we live, we need our renowned colleges and graduate schools to produce highly educated engineers, scientists and doctors, but not everyone is qualified for such training. Although we spend adequate amounts and work to improve the teaching of math and science in our high schools for all students, we do not turn out enough high quality students prepared to move on to college or a community college. Many teachers in inner city schools are hindered by having a large number of students who require extra help and often disrupt the education of the remainder of the class. We should be supporting more high schools like New York City's Bronx High School of Science to educate our most capable students to give them the opportunity to learn the fundamentals required to design the high tech products needed to keep America great. We should also change our immigration laws to permit foreign students graduating from our colleges and graduate schools to remain permanently in the US and to give permanent immigration visas to foreigners desiring to open a well-capitalized business in the US.

College education despite its many recognized benefits has become very costly. Colleges have taken advantage of the availability of student loans to raise tuition charges. College education for a large percentage of students is overrated. The benefits often fail to justify the cost. Students who are left with large outstanding student loan obligations often learn very few specific job skills. Unless college students find good paying jobs after graduation or more scholarships are offered, college enrollment will inevitably begin to decline.

President Obama talks about offering at least one year of community college for all students, but he certainly can't mean that we should offer such training for those students who never achieve above fifth or sixth grade level. If we grow our economy, we will create jobs for young people with limited book learning abilities. Many of them can learn trades and find good paying jobs where they can improve their skills. They can learn math and language skills from their day-to-day experience.

On-line colleges offer students the opportunity to learn at their own convenience at greatly reduced cost while working at a full or part time job. The best teachers could reach large numbers of students on-line throughout the world. Many self-motivated students might be better off taking one or two courses on-line while going to trade schools that teach job oriented skills suited for industries with job openings.

For example job opportunities are available for workers, including high school graduates, willing to relocate to North

Dakota and capable of learning the required skills on the job to fill high paying jobs in the rapidly expanding oil drilling business using modern fracking procedures. Naturally, employers prefer to hire well-trained and experienced employees. However, as often happens in rapidly growing high tech businesses or businesses where environmental concerns are of utmost priority there aren't enough trained employees available. Employers have learned that they often must find a way to provide supplemental on-the-job training and teach safety procedures to all employees. As the boomtowns grow there is a demand for workers to meet housing, retail, medical, teaching and local government needs.

Those who have lost jobs, college graduates, young people seeking to join the workforce (even those with inadequate grade school education), military personnel returning from war and seniors who have lost a substantial portion of their wealth and can't afford to retire, need jobs. We must find a way to jump-start and grow the economy to generate over a five year period the more than twenty million jobs needed to provide an opportunity for everyone wanting to work. We will also need almost two million additional meaningful jobs every year thereafter as the potential work force grows, so that every American able and willing to work can have the opportunity to enjoy the American dream and have the opportunity for upward mobility. If we do so we will (i) generate a meaningful and self-sustainable upturn in our economy, (ii) generate the tax revenues needed to finance our federal and state government expenditures, (iii) stabilize the national debt and (iv) permit us to honor all of our burdensome entitlements if they are realistically modified, without runaway inflation.

It is a mammoth task. It is going to require us to modernize our infrastructure, reverse the housing decline and create new industries some of which are suggested here and others that will be generated by imaginative new business ideas and technology advances. As our economy grows, our businesses will begin to hire additional employees in good paying jobs to meet the growing demand for their products and services.

Instead of attacking families and the rich and confiscating wealth with unfair tax increases, we must find ways to get the holders of our private wealth to invest it in ways to promote job creation and economic expansion. Our cash-rich businesses and individuals can be given the opportunity to help our economically stressed states finance transportation infrastructure projects. Transportation infrastructure funding from the sale of Jump Start America Bonds discussed below is a good place to start.

Sale of Transportation Infrastructure Construction and Industrial Bonds to be known as Jump Start America Bonds

We have various US Government programs aimed at helping our states finance road, bridge, tunnel and other transportation infrastructure construction projects planned by the states and their transportation agencies. Our initially high quality but aging and in some cases outmoded interstate highway system was developed and maintained in this manner. It created many thousands of jobs, facilitated personal travel and business transportation and led to years of wealth creation and growth in the GDP. Maintaining and enhancing our transportation system has provided continuous construction jobs nationally.

Unfortunately, in recent years we have not adequately funded the maintenance and upgrading of our interstate transportation infrastructure. Most of our states and cities, which play a vital role in selecting, overseeing and financing our infrastructure projects, were devastated by the Great Recession and have serious budgetary constraints. They must devote a substantial portion of funds available for transportation construction to the repair of state highways and local roads. They have high priority projects which if funded would generate hundreds of thousands of construction jobs. They need assistance from the federal government or outside sources to finance these needed projects. President Obama's stimulus program did not allocate adequate funding for transportation infrastructure construction projects and included some poorly chosen earmarked construction projects.

During his campaign travels across the country, President Obama made speeches about the availability of Department of Transportation (DOT) funding to promote infrastructure projects nationwide. Like almost everything the US Government gets involved in at the current time the DOT, which runs the TIFIA program, is highly politicized and its funding is constrained by our gridlocked Congress. During 2012 it allocated funding across the country in too many cases as political favors to get votes for President Obama and other Democratic candidates. In April 2012, the DOT approved $13 billion of loans to fund what appear on their face to be worthwhile projects mostly in closely contested swing states, but such amount is a small fraction of what is needed.

The Department of Transportation concurrently rejected a $2 billion loan request from the State of New York to fund a portion of the then expected more than $5 billion cost to double the size of the Tappan Zee Bridge, which has for many years exceeded its capacity usage and had safety concerns. Approval of the loan, which was denied on the grounds that insufficient funds were available to the DOT, should have been a no-brainer. Its long delayed construction will initially create thousands of jobs in an area with a large number of unemployed construction workers and bring benefits to NYC and other cities on both sides of the Hudson River, as well as to the individuals and business entities that rely on the bridge, which is a major crossing point to and from upstate New York and New England. The ability to repay the cost of building it within a reasonable time period is virtually assured based on current and expected growth of usage. The State of New York has recently been discussing financing the bridge with funds borrowed from the New York State Pension Fund. That is not a good idea because of the interest rate risk of the investment.

A significant number of transportation related construction projects of this type carried out on a national basis would help jump-start the US economy. However, our deadlocked Congress, frightened by the failure of the President's $830 billion stimulus plan and other stimulus efforts (including the hundreds of billions of dollars of withholding tax reductions) and the soaring national debt, has failed to approve adequate transportation infrastructure funding. The 2012 DOT spending authorization was almost two billion dollars below the prior year's amount. The transportation bill should have added at least two hundred billion dollars to TIFIA spending over such period, but President Obama had wasted his political capital and refuses even to discuss bringing entitlement spending under control.

We must find a way for private entities and individuals to assist in jump-starting our economy. It is time for us to end the attacks on corporations for not bringing home the $1.7 trillion they have in overseas accounts largely for tax reasons, and class warfare against the individuals who pay the lion's share of federal and state income taxes. We must modify our federal income tax laws to encourage businesses and individuals to join in the effort to perpetuate American greatness by investing to promote job creation needed to jump-start our economy and lead it to sustainable long-term growth. One way is to create a new type of transportation infrastructure construction and industrial bonds known as Jump Start America Bonds.

We should change the federal and state tax laws as necessary to permit the sale of a new class of bonds - Jump Start America Bonds issued by states or state agencies. Jump Start America Bonds will be sold to finance major transportation construction projects nationwide. Jump Start America Bonds would be similar in most respects to tax exempt bonds issued by our states, but would have special characteristics and new federal tax benefits to encourage their purchase. Jump Start America Bonds will be designed to attract investments from corporations including those with un-repatriated overseas profits and from wealthy Americans.

The US Government has in the past without appreciative success offered temporary tax relief to enable entities to bring home funds held offshore in the hope they would make capital investments in the US. The problem was that capital investments are generally made only by entities that perceive they will profit by producing and selling additional products and services. Most of the entities with cash parked overseas had no need for additional US based capacity and didn't invest the repatriated funds in ways to increase productive capacity or jobs. Similar conditions remain today.

Instead of offering tax relief to entities to bring home offshore funds and enable them to use it to improve their balance sheet or pay dividends and redeem stock (which in all likelihood would offer only minimal stimulus), we can offer our international corporate entities the opportunity to help our country build a sustainable soundly financed recovery while allowing them to concurrently resolve in whole or in part their troubling outstanding offshore tax problems and earn a reasonable and safe return on such funds.

To encourage their purchase, the principal invested in such Jump Start America Bonds by entities should be deemed to remain offshore but the tax free interest earned should be treated as returned to the US and a portion of each interest payment should be withheld to pay outstanding federal tax obligations based on the offshore profits of the holders at significantly discounted rates such as 1/3 of the current tax rate, to encourage investments. We could alternatively require all of the interest received to be treated as a tax payment and permit the holder of the bond to repatriate additional funds which when added to the tax payment would have given rise to the tax liability paid.

Although the bonds would be liabilities of the states and not guaranteed by the US Government (which guaranty might be difficult to get Congress to approve) we can offer the investors important benefits, including (i) protection against loss by offering the Jump Start America Bond Trustee a standard type of security interest in the revenues generated from designated high quality projects and (ii) granting the holders of Jump Start America Bonds who are entities the right at any time beginning 5 years after issuance, prior to or after default, to apply the principal of the bonds at their face amount plus accrued interest in payment toward the corporate holder's federal tax liabilities of any kind. In such event we might treat 20% or more of such principal amount as having been repatriated to the US and subject to tax at the substantially discounted rates. The portion deemed repatriated might be phased out as the holding period increases. The five-year holding requirement might not apply to bonds tendered to pay off shore tax liabilities at the substantially discounted rates.

Upon tendering the Jump Start America Bonds to be applied in payment of the holder's offshore tax liabilities due on repatriation at the discounted rate, the holder would be entitled to return to the US an additional amount which when added to the tax paid would have given rise to such tax payment.

By allowing the Jump Start America Bonds to be tendered at their face value by entities in payment of federal income taxes on both US based and offshore earned profits, we would be removing the holder's risk of loss resulting from states' defaults or adverse interest rate changes.

We might consider giving further protection to investors by having the US Government offer a completion bond that provides that if the project is not completed by an outside date or if other progress points are not met, the project will be taken over and completed by the US Army Corps of Engineers at a cost to be added to the cost of the project and paid to the US Government by the issuance of additional project bonds, which will be subordinate to the Jump Start America Bonds.

To encourage the purchase of Jump Start America Bonds by wealthy individuals we should change the Federal Estate Tax Laws to enable individual holders of Jump Start America Bonds the opportunity to use the bonds at face value like previously issued "Flower Bonds" to pay Federal Estate Taxes. By allowing the use of bonds issued by state governments (and their agencies) to pay Federal Estate Taxes at what may effectively be a discount and eliminating the risk of loss of principal, the Federal government would be giving assistance to the states in raising capital for infrastructure spending. Flower Bonds had to be owned by the decedent at the time of death. We should include a similar requirement. Because of the income tax revenue received by the IRS from the GDP growth resulting from the sale of the bonds, we might consider offering a premium on the delivery to the US Treasury in payment of Federal Estate Taxes of Jump Start America Bonds held for a designated time period, such as five years.

Bonds would be transferrable so that entities wishing to repatriate overseas funds and pay the tax due at the then discounted rate or individuals facing imminent death and estate tax payments would be encouraged to purchase Jump Start America Bonds. Such purchases would bid up the price for such bonds, lowering the interest rate at which such bonds could be offered by the states.

The sale of the project specific Jump Start America Bonds would be approved in advance by the DOT. Because (i) funding of all or a substantial portion of the project is private, (ii) the US exposure is limited to the collection of reduced tax payments (some of which it might not receive for many years, if ever), and (iii) the US Government can expect to receive tax payments and other benefits from the growth in the GDP resulting from the sale of the bonds, the DOT approval should be almost automatic and not politically motivated. We should require the DOT to accept a finding made in the reasonable discretion of the state submitting the approval request to the DOT that the project is necessary and financially viable.

Our international corporations have a presence across the US and are well aware of the local infrastructure needs. There is the potential for hundreds of billions of dollars to be made available nationwide within a year or two to supplement the funds available to the states to finance many projects that are or near shovel ready. These bonds would help bring the run-down and outdated US infrastructure into the 21st Century by funding bridge, tunnel, highway, and possibly railroad and airport improvements across the US. Such projects would be expected in a short time period to create more than a hundred thousand construction jobs and an equal number of secondary jobs in the vicinity of the projects. The new jobs will jump start GDP growth and the sale of housing and housing related products in the vicinity of the construction sites.

Changing the tax laws to encourage the Jump Start America Bond offerings will create a win, win, win (i) for the investing entities and wealthy individuals from the growth of the US economy, from safe investment income protected against loss of principal, from tax savings (including from a potential change in the federal tax laws to tax overseas income) and from the good-will that will flow from the investment, (ii) for the states and state agencies that will benefit from the funding and revenues and other benefits derived from the completed project and the construction activity and (iii) for the federal government that will benefit from the tax revenues generated from the offshore tax payments and the income and other tax payments from the project's employees, the growth of the GDP and reduced unemployment related payments.

Perhaps the most important benefit that the investing entities and individuals will receive from the purchase of Jump Start America Bonds will be the personal satisfaction of being part of a group of patriotic Americans helping our country. Investors will also benefit from the favorable publicity they will get from their contribution to job creation and prosperity on our shores. We could offer a further incentive to invest by naming the Jump Start America Bond issue or the road or bridge to be constructed with the Jump Start America Bond proceeds after the entity or individual supplying a major portion or all of the funding. We might also create an honor roll of corporations and individuals purchasing large amounts such as $10 Million or more of Jump Start America Bonds.

The financial press, President Obama, governors, Congressmen and mayors should be eager to promote the sale of Jump Start America Bonds. Instead of unfair and excessive taxes on hard working individuals to pay for the past mistakes of our federal and state governments that are promoting class warfare, we can reach out to our cash rich corporations and individuals to invest in growing the American economy.

Characteristics of a Jump Start America Bond

1. The Jump Start America Bond would be issued by a state or state agency and contain standard type provisions required to protect the investors. Because the specific transaction terms would in most cases be negotiated with sophisticated investors the bond and related bond indenture would in most cases not have to be registered with the SEC. However, the bonds would probably be registered with the SEC to enable a market to develop and improve transferability. The issuer would attempt to identify a corporate or individual sponsor for all or a portion of the offering while the project is being finalized and prior to effectiveness of the Registration Statement or commencement of the offering.

2. The Jump Start America Bonds would pay federal, state and city tax-free interest payable semi-annually, but would not be guaranteed by the US government. The interest rate should be similar to (and might even be lower than) US government guaranteed bonds of equal maturity dates because of the tax and other advantages offered to holders.

3. The payment of interest and principal on the Jump Start America Bonds shall be secured by the tolls or fees generated from the specifically identified construction project.

4. The bond would have a term of 5 to 35 years with the length calculated to permit interest payments and the repayment in full of the principal from a sinking fund generated from the conservatively estimated portion of the revenue of

the project allocated to the Jump Start America Bond. The initial interest payments during the construction period will have to be included in the amount raised or otherwise provided for. Lengthening the term of the bond will reduce the toll increase necessary to meet the bond payment requirements. If the completion of the project is delayed, we could give the state the option to add specified interest and principal payments and penalties within stated limits to the end of the term. Principal pre-payments will be made from time to time from funds available in the sinking fund. The states or their agencies will retain ownership of the road, bridge or tunnel. Upon repayment of the Jump Start America Bonds, all future net revenues from the road, bridge or tunnel will belong to the state or its agency.

5. The payment of the interest on a Jump Start America Bond to an entity with an offshore income tax obligation on repatriation would be made to the holder and treated as a repatriation of such payment to the US. A portion of the interest on the bond would be withheld and paid directly to the US Treasury for the benefit of the registered owner to be applied in payment of the investing entity's tax obligation due based upon the repatriation to the US of the interest payment. The investor's outstanding tax obligation for each payment shall be payable at a specified reduced rate, approximately one-third of the current rate. The holder would be permitted to repatriate the remainder of the interest payment after deducting the portion withheld. Alternatively, we could treat the entire interest payment as a payment of the repatriation tax at the reduced rate and enable the entity to repatriate to the US an amount that would have given rise to such tax payment.

6. The principal amount of the Jump Start America Bonds would be repaid to the investing entity offshore.

7. The Jump Start America Bond would include an option to enable the holder to apply any part of the principal at face value plus accrued interest at any time beginning five years (or such longer period as determined by Congress) after the issuance of the Jump Start America Bond (before or after default or maturity) to either of the following:

(i) If the holder is an entity, to the (i) payment of any tax due to the IRS or (ii) repayment of its offshore tax payable on repatriation to the US at a specified discount, which would be established by the legislation authorizing the tax treatment of the Jump Start America Bonds and fixed for the term of the bond, but might be modified annually by Congress for future bond offerings. If the principal of the Jump Start America Bond is applied in payment of a tax obligation other than to the tax due on the repatriation of overseas profits 20% of such amount shall be treated as having been repatriated to the US and be taxable at the substantially discounted rate. The portion subject to such tax might be phased out as the holding period of the bond increases; or

(ii) If the holder is the estate of an individual who owned the Jump Start America Bond at death, to the payment of the Federal Estate Tax due. In such event, the five-year holding period would not apply.

8. Jump Start America Bonds transferred to the US Treasury in payment of taxes would become an asset of the US Treasury, which would step into the rights of the holder.

9. The Jump Start America Bonds would be transferrable.

Jump Start America Bonds could also be used by the US government to create hundreds of thousands of jobs by funding a large number of projects as well as new and expanded public or joint public-private ventures which would appeal to potential offshore or onshore bond investors, including:

1. Large-scale water desalination and purification projects and interstate water pipelines (the "Interstate Aqueduct").

   A shortage of drinking water is going to be a problem during the first half of this century. We should build water desalination plants located at facilities on our shorelines or on ships docked off coastal ports. The water will be delivered via the Interstate Aqueduct and stored in reservoirs at appropriate locations to meet domestic water needs, to promote farming, to help control wind fires and to be exported as needed worldwide. Excess rainwater can be added to the reservoirs. The desalination plants and pipeline would be built and owned by a series of private companies under permits from the US government that could be capitalized like the limited partnerships that currently build and own the oil and gas pipelines across the country.

   The financial viability of this project in the near term will depend on the ability of the entity undertaking the project to enter into firm future contracts for the sale of the water to be transported over the Interstate Aqueduct. This may be difficult because it is impossible to predict weather conditions from year to year. A futures market for water will have to be developed for potential purchasers of the water wishing to hedge their needs or speculate on the demand for water.

2. Fire control systems.

   Billions of dollars are lost each year to forest fires and other fires spread by wind. We can grant licenses to private (or combined public and private) entities to build and maintain complex sprinkler systems using desalinated water from the Interstate Aqueduct to control wind and forest fires and to protect high risk residential areas and offer the sprinkler service at a charge to property owners.

3. Promoting Home Mortgage Refinancing.

   USHOMECORP, the entity to be created under the Federal Mortgage Law proposed herein, could resolve mortgage issues and help revive housing construction.

4. Building hotels to promote tourism.

   We can promote jobs and tourism by offering leases to world-class international hotel entities to construct environmentally safe five star hotels with a limited number of rooms inside our national parks. This will create large numbers of construction jobs and promote international tourism throughout the US, creating additional jobs and helping our balance of payments.

5. Building a network of communication towers and protection of cyberspace.

   We can create an entity to expand, and regulate a national network of communication towers owned by or licensed to our current tower owners or our communication entities. We can provide protection of cyberspace from hackers and terrorist activity and charge the communication tower owners and users for the cost.

6. Upgrading, expanding and protecting the electric power grid.

   We can create an entity to upgrade, expand, and protect the electric power grid and charge utilities and ultimately consumers for the cost.

7. Fencing our ports.

We can create an entity to modernize and fence our ports and neighboring areas and have the Department of Customs or the Department of Homeland Security employ returning veterans to prevent terrorists from entering the US. We can reasonably increase landing fees and offer retail space for rental within the fenced areas to pay for a portion of the cost of modernizing and fencing the ports.

As Jump Start America Bonds are paid off from the revenues of successful projects, investors with offshore tax liabilities can be expected to rollover the principal payments received from Jump Start America Bonds in new bonds then being offered.

Jump Start America Bonds might also be attractive to the millionaires and billionaires that President Obama has unfairly demonized. They might be interested in stepping up and investing in Jump Start America Bonds because of their desire to help participate in a sustainable recovery that will benefit all Americans.

THE PLIGHT OF OUR STATES AND CITIES

Long before the Great Recession, a majority of our states and cities used long-term borrowing practices to pay current obligations and became highly overleveraged and overcommitted to future obligations they could not realistically expect to be able to pay. It was inevitable that over time without significant inflation or significant growth in the GDP that would have increased tax revenues, a substantial portion of the promised benefits could not be afforded. Rising public employee compensation and costs of providing for needs of the poor forced them to neglect infrastructure spending, which resulted in insufficient maintenance and upgrading of roads, bridges and tunnels.

The Great Recession that deflated housing values and significantly reduced the revenue of states, cities and municipalities from both income and real estate taxes and filing fees has accelerated the timing of the problem and has left many of them in a position where they are struggling to meet their current obligations or will not be able to meet their future obligations to their employees. Many state and city retirement plans are underfunded and use unreasonable income projections.

The states, cities and municipalities have differing fiscal problems and many are attempting to deal with their financial issues now because of current difficulties or to avert an inevitable crisis in the future. Like southern European countries, our states cannot print money to pay their bills and many have exhausted their borrowing power. Although the upturn in the GDP has led to moderately increased tax revenues for states, cities and municipalities, most states continue to use budgetary tricks to pay for necessary services and balance their budgets because public employee salaries, healthcare and retirement obligations are increasing much faster than revenues.

Areas such as the industrial mid-west or states such as Arizona, California, Florida and Georgia have been hardest hit because of joblessness or collapsing housing prices. These states and their cities and municipalities in an attempt to balance their budgets have (i) cut construction and other nonessential spending, leading to lost public construction jobs and deteriorating roads, bridges and tunnels and (ii) reluctantly reduced the number of teachers, policemen, firemen and other employees often by eliminating positions like music and art teachers and librarians and not filling positions vacated by retirees.

Public employee unions have for more than 50 years used strikes and threats of strikes and the promise of political support for corrupt politicians to negotiate (or in too many cases extort) contractually excessive compensation and benefits. Unionized public employees now make substantially more income and are entitled to much more favorable healthcare and pension benefits while making lesser contributions than private sector employees. The total compensation excess of public sector employees over private sector employees in the same communities often exceeds 30%. The Democratic party has over the years gained recognition and votes as a supporter of the demands of organized labor.

Strikes by public employee unions should never have been permitted. The contracts they claim they "negotiated" are jeopardizing the solvency of many states, cities and municipalities. Almost all governors and mayors are attempting to deal with serious financial problems. However, one can observe that as a general rule the states and cities governed by Democrats seem more concerned with retaining or increasing the excessive wages and health care and retirement benefits of their unionized employees and seeking other avenues, such as tax increases, to resolve the financial crisis they face.

The public employee unions have been generally unwilling to meaningfully renegotiate any employment or pension benefits that they claim they bargained for. Many think unrealistically that with an upturn in the economy the problem caused by their excess compensation and benefits will go away. That is not going to happen, even with exceptional GDP growth. The spread between the commitments of most of our states and cities over their likely revenue sources is too great.

President Obama has generally ignored the plight of our states and cities, which are required by their state constitutions to balance their budgets. Obamacare, although giving the states a subsidy to cover their increased Medicaid costs in the early years as an inducement to accept it, greatly increases future state Medicaid obligations.

Some states have passed laws or changed rules regarding public employees' pension and health care benefits that are being challenged in the courts, by recall elections and the nominating of candidates who favor the union positions. In an attempt to obtain labor union support for his reelection, President Obama, in total disregard for the solvency of the states, has sided with the union position in too many confrontations over excess compensation and benefits. He senses an opportunity to have elected Republican representatives removed from or voted out of office and replaced by Democrats. This is just another example of President Obama taking a political stance to gain votes and reward friends and supporters rather than doing what is right for our country by helping or permitting the states to deal with their financial problems.

There is a limit to the ability of cities and states to control costs and still provide vital services. We can expect that unless there is a surge in the GDP many of our cities and even some states will face bankruptcy and require financial assistance within ten years.

INCOME TAX FAIRNESS

President Obama made tax fairness that is highly subjective an important campaign issue. He has socialistic views of tax fairness. He confused the issues. He talked about taking a little more from millionaires but that statement was deliberately misleading. His principle proposal for dealing with the Fiscal Cliff was to eliminate the Bush tax cuts for families earning over $250,000 and individuals earning over $200,000 whom he calls rich even though he knows that if they live in a large metropolitan city they are probably not rich. He knew, but disregarded the fact that the amount of the additional tax revenue he demanded was meaningless in solving the federal deficit problem.

He ignored that fact that he had already included similar type of taxes on income from the same group of taxpayers as part of Obamacare. He also managed to induce Congress to reduce the tax deductions on most of these taxpayers under the American Taxpayer Relief Act of 2012 to effectively increase their tax rate. How many times do you have to raise the taxes on the same group of taxpayers a little bit more before it becomes a lot more?

Early in his reelection campaign he attacked Governor Romney for paying only about 15% of his income in taxes. His supporter Warren Buffett publicized the fact that he paid a lower tax rate than his secretary. Governor Romney and Mr. Buffett pay such lower rate because they have large charitable deductions and municipal bond, dividend and capital gains income. President Obama didn't talk about the merits of the tax provisions that offer lower tax rates on dividends and capital gains, which are arguably unfair and were increased from 15% to 20% under the American Taxpayer Relief Act of 2012, and up to an additional 3.8% under Obamacare. These lower rates arguably encourage investment and have a large number of supporters.

President Obama's disgraceful demagoguery, which included attacks by his supporters on Governor Romney's personal low tax rate, was designed to create class jealousy and to make him appear to be the champion of the middle class and the poor. No evidence was disclosed that might indicate that Governor Romney has not paid all required tax payments under the current tax law.

President Obama deliberately confused the issues relating to tax fairness. He misled many voters into thinking that all taxpayers earning over $200,000 and families earning over $250,000 pay only about 15% of their income in taxes. Most of them were paying a much higher rate. He failed to distinguish between individuals who earned $200,000 or more and under the Bush tax cuts were paying marginal federal and state income tax rates totaling almost 40% of their income and those earning over a million dollars a year and had marginal federal and state income tax rates from 15% to 20%.

There was a strong argument that individuals earning over $200,000 and families earning over $250,000 from personal services except those taking advantage of a loophole discussed below even with the benefits of the Bush tax cuts were already paying more than their fair share of the federal and state income taxes. Half of all taxpayers were and still are paying no federal income taxes or receive a negative income tax.

Despite President Obama's obfuscating statements about rich people paying only 15% of their income in federal income taxes, even with the benefit of the Bush tax cuts, taxpayers were paying marginal federal income taxes at a rate of 33% (or for many taxpayers about 40% including state income tax) on all income in excess of $217,450 and 35% on incomes in excess of $388,350. This maximum rate will be supplemented by up to 4.7% as a result of new income taxes included in the Obamacare legislation for individual taxpayers with employment income above $200,000 and families with employment income above $250,000 with substantial investment income. By comparison families with taxable income of between $17,400 and $70,700 have a marginal Federal tax rate of 15% established by the Bush tax cuts and they will pay no additional tax under Obamacare. Thus, in 2012 the marginal tax rates paid by individuals earning over $200,000 and families earning over $250,000 greatly exceeded the low marginal tax rates of low-income taxpayers. Taxpayers are discovering that Democrats introduced a second and parallel federal income tax to help fund Obamacare that they treat as a health care tax. The marginal federal tax rate on individuals earning over $400,000 and families earning over $450,000 (and $225,000 for married individuals filing separately) has become even higher 39.6%) under the American Taxpayer Relief Act of 2012.

A claim by President Obama that families with annual income of $250,000 who live in the large metropolitan areas such as NY, LA, Boston, Dallas and Chicago are rich is a deliberately misleading misstatement. It was made for political gain by promoting jealousy or arguments among the classes. It was intended to appeal to voters in the lower income groups (approximately half of all Americans), including those who are retired and living on social security benefits or benefitting from welfare programs.

Under President Obama's tax proposals as adopted some taxpayers with family incomes above $450,000 will be paying a Federal marginal income tax rate of almost 43% on incomes over $450,000, or an increase of almost 20% over their 2012 marginal federal income tax rate. This is hardly the small increase that President Obama talked about. The rate is effectively higher because of deductions disallowed to these taxpayers under the American Taxpayer Relief Act of 2012. In some cases the combined Federal and state marginal income tax rate (including the Obamacare tax) will equal approximately 50% of taxable income. Of course not everyone having those levels of taxable income will also have the amount of employment income or investment income needed to maximize their rates. Maybe this is the revenge President Obama promised in a campaign speech if you voted for him.

It does not bode well for the survival of American capitalism that a president can get elected relying on the votes of people who pay no income taxes based on a promise that he will raise the taxes of people he calls rich even if they are middle class. In most major cities families with incomes of $250,000 are struggling to pay their bills and unable to save for retirement or for college tuitions for their children (who are not eligible for scholarships based on need), and are at best upper middle class. President Obama knows this, but believed correctly that it would gain votes from his base.

President Obama's concern about tax fairness obviously does not apply to families. Both Obamacare and the American Taxpayer Relief Act of 2012 have outrageous provisions which tax married couples unfairly. The Medicare Contribution Tax introduced under Obamacare places a new 3.8% tax on the lesser of adjusted gross income above a threshold ($200,000 for individuals and $250,000 for a married couple filing jointly, $125,000 for a married individual filing separately) and a highly complex definition of investment income which includes interest, dividends, capital gains, annuities, rents and royalties and certain large gains on the sale of a residence. The Obamacare income tax may prove difficult to interpret and it is a harbinger of President Obama's and liberal Democrat's future plans to increase taxes on a broad range of income. The new .9% FICA Hospital Insurance Payroll Tax included in the Obamacare legislation has the same threshold of $250,000 for a married couple ($125,000 for a married couple filing separately) but $200,000 for an individual who is not married.

Thus, Obamacare creates a large and unfair marriage penalty. Married couples with aggregate incomes that exceed $250,000 have a lower exemption threshold for the Obamacare taxes than two individuals (who may be living together) who earn up to $200,000 each. For example if two working spouses each earn $175,000 of employment income and they have combined investment income of $100,000 they pay the new taxes on $100,000 ($350,000-$250,000) of income or a total of $4,700 under Obamacare while two unmarried individuals, each earning $175,000, living separately or together do not pay the Obamacare taxes.

The income tax changes under the American Taxpayer Relief Act of 2012 are even more egregiously unfair to married couples. For example two individuals living together and earning $400,000 and $350,000 respectively escape the tax increase under the act. On the other hand if they are married they pay an additional income tax at the reinstated Clinton tax rate of 39.6% which is 4.6%, or $13,800, higher on their income over $450,000. They cannot escape the marriage penalty by filing singly because the threshold for married individuals filing singly is $225,000.

The American Taxpayer Relief Act of 2012 is so unfair to married couples that it should be challenged as unconstitutional. Why has the financial press ignored the unfairness of the tax changes? Some married couples may consider getting divorced as part of their income tax planning.

When talking about tax fairness, President Obama never presented a schedule comparing current rates for all taxpayers and the effective rates if the Bush tax cuts were eliminated. President Obama never talked about the fact that half of our families pay no income tax or receive negative income tax benefits. Before the adoption of Obamacare and the American Taxpayer Relief Act of 2012 taxpayers who were earning over $250,000 were paying a very substantial portion of all income taxes and taxpayers with the 20% highest incomes were paying over 90% of all income taxes.

Note that by targeting millionaires and billionaires in his demagoguery and not people with annual incomes over $1,000,000 he is expanding his attack on the rich to one on accumulated wealth. President Obama's blunderbuss attack on asset ownership was designed to gain votes for reelection and is a dangerous step toward socialism. Since the American colonies gained independence, working hard to accumulate wealth has been the cornerstone of American greatness. Wealth that may be owned in the form of buildings, businesses, stocks and bonds, homes, art work, sports cars or farms is often illiquid and has never been taxed in the US except under the gift or estate tax. Spending by wealthy Americans to purchase and maintain multiple homes, planes, collectibles and cars, which many socialists find excessive and unnecessary, creates millions of jobs.

President Obama's argument that the US government needed additional revenue and that no one should have objected to going back to the Clinton era tax rates overlooked the fact that President Obama was not looking to let the Bush tax cuts expire for everyone including lower income taxpayers. Although the Bush tax cuts were originally proposed based on an ill-conceived premise to give the excess government income back to the taxpayers, by the time they were passed they were in effect a Keynesian stimulus which helped under the then existing conditions to offset the decline in the US economy following the collapse of the .com bubble in the last year of the Clinton Presidency. The argument that we should not remove the stimulus of the Bush tax cuts for families earning less than $250,000 because it would negatively impact consumer spending applied equally to the effect removal of the Bush tax cuts would have on most families earning less than $500,000 or even higher.

Although high-income taxpayers pay a large percentage of all taxes, we have long recognized the fairness and appropriateness of graduated tax brackets. The Bush tax cuts increased the steepness of marginal rates. The Obamacare income taxes and the American Taxpayer Relief Act of 2012 further increased the steepness of the tax rate curve.

The higher taxes imposed by the American Taxpayer Relief Act of 2012 may result in lesser investment and hiring by small business and prove to be counterproductive. Since taxpayers earning over $200,000 and families earning over $250.000 were already facing an income tax increase under Obamacare, the American Taxpayer Relief Act of 2012 could have left the marginal income tax rate for individuals earning under $500,000 and families earning under $1,000,000 unchanged or it could have eliminated only a portion of the Bush income tax cuts for such taxpayers. It could have established a new tax bracket for families with taxable income over $1,000,000 (and for individuals with income over $500,000), which might have increased the marginal tax rate to Clinton tax levels. Even such a change might have discouraged business investment.

Some would argue that the highest marginal tax rates for individuals were much higher under past presidents. After adjusting for inflation such higher marginal rates were at higher income levels. When rates were higher taxpayers sought losses from investments financed with non-recourse indebtedness and looked for ways to convert ordinary income into capital gains. Confiscatory tax rates would be stifling to job creation and economic growth.

The proposed supply side income tax cuts proposed by Governor Romney to be offset by reduced credits and deductions were little more likely than President Obama's to promote capital investment and job growth or to end the housing crisis.

Governor Romney never spelled out how he would reduce deductions, so it was impossible to discuss the tax fairness of his proposal.

Some conservatives have proposed eliminating most deductions and installing a flat tax on individuals at low rates and reduced corporate tax rates. Others argue we should reduce the number of brackets.

The Federal income tax code has been reviewed annually to make adjustments to improve it. However, in recent years Congress has failed to deal with major tax loopholes. Our country has a history of making a major revision in the tax code about every 25 years with the last such revision coming in 1986. Certainly in 2012 year, with so many automatic changes scheduled to come into effect in 2013, Congress should have attempted to close the major loopholes and reviewed the appropriate brackets and rates following an open bi-partisan debate in Congress.

Both President Obama and the Republicans missed the real tax fairness argument based on the fact that many of our highest income taxpayers earning tens of millions or in some cases billions of dollars per year have most of their income taxed at capital gains rates (15% in 2012 and now 20%) and not the much higher ordinary income rates. They are using tax loopholes to amass great fortunes in payment for their personal services while paying federal income taxes at a rate reserved for the capital that they are managing for investors. The rationale behind lower tax rates for capital gains is that the taxpayer is investing after tax dollars and we want to encourage investments to be made in the US to create economic growth and jobs. The disparity in tax rates will be partly reduced by the scheduled increase in long-term capital gains rates from 15% to 20% at the end of 2012, which met little opposition even though capital gains of some taxpayers will also be subject to a 3.8% Obamacare tax beginning in 2013.

The reason for the low tax rate is that a large part of the income of our highest earning taxpayers is in the form of a carried interest. The percentage of the profits, which becomes the carried interest of private equity and hedge fund managers and the income share of the general partners of real estate and oil and gas pipeline partnerships, is under the federal tax laws relating to partnerships and LLCs treated in the same manner as the income earned by other partners. However, it is not income earned from their invested capital but is a payment for services for managing the invested capital of others being taxed under current law at capital gains rates.

Although it has been a long-standing rule that partners can in their discretion allocate income among the partners, the carried interest of investment partnerships should be treated as a management fee and treated as ordinary income and taxed as such. Taxing the carried interest of private equity, hedge fund and partnership managements at ordinary tax rates should be a "no-brainer" which will raise many billions of dollars and although few people talk about it, the tax laws should have been changed years ago to promote tax fairness. One reason that the carried interest loophole has not been dealt with is that individuals and entities benefitting from the current laws are large contributors to the politicians of both parties.

Cash flow issues relating to the change in taxing the carried interest can be resolved by giving a manager, partner or officer who earns a vested interest in profits of an entity the option (i) to defer the calculation and payment of the tax on his profit participation until the interest becomes liquid (or for a defined or maximum period of time such as 5 or 10 years) or (ii) to pay the tax on his profit when it becomes vested and receive a basis and holding period for that portion of his interest the further appreciation of which would then be eligible for capital gains treatment. For equity in securities listed on a national exchange, we might give the taxpayer the option to pay the tax in kind if permitted by the entity. The asset received by the IRS can be sold by the IRS over time.

Arguments that increasing the tax rate for investment managers will discourage capital formation and job creation ignore the fact that few investment managers with an opportunity to make tens or hundreds of millions of dollars of compensation will not form an entity or fail to accept a management position because they have to pay fair ordinary income tax rates. Nor will many of them move out of the US and renounce their US citizenship.

There is talk emanating from both parties urging the simplification of the tax code by eliminating deductions or credits that were included in the tax code for valid social reasons or to stimulate the economy. Using tax deductions to promote home ownership and charitable giving have long been recognized as desirable. Mortgage deductions (including 2nd home mortgages) and property tax deductions are more needed now that home ownership is endangered than ever before in our history. Many liberal democrats and talk show hosts argue that home ownership gets favorable treatment over apartment renters because of the mortgage and state and local tax deductions that are not available to renters. That is not a valid argument. Landlords can charge less rent because they can deduct mortgage interest and real estate tax payments and have the added benefit of depreciation expense unavailable to homeowners.

Congress found a stealth way to greatly reduce itemized deductions for individuals earning above $250,000 and families earning above $300,000. The American Taxpayer Relief Act of 2012 reduces the itemized deductions by adding a little discussed tax provision phasing out up to 80% of itemized deductions for individuals earning above $250,000 and families earning above $300,000. The phase out occurs over the first $125,000 of additional income. The provision is another example of unfair taxation of middle class families.

The Alternative Minimum Tax was originally added to create tax fairness. Many middle class taxpayers have because of the effects of inflation over time become subject to the alternative minimum tax. Although permanent relief from the Alternative Minimum tax has been given to some taxpayers under the American Taxpayer Relief Act of 2012, the middle class did not receive adequate relief. On the other hand Congress should have considered taxing dividends and capital gains in excess of a million dollars under the alternative minimum tax.

Our corporate tax rates are among the highest in the world. Both parties have a plan to reduce corporate tax rates but they would eliminate some corporate tax credits and deductions to offset the proposed benefits. There is an obvious inequity in Federal and state corporate taxation that results in some corporations paying 40% of their income in taxes and others avoiding or deferring almost all of their tax payments. That doesn't mean we should thoughtlessly take an ax to all credits and deductions some of which are important to encourage investment and job creation. We could provide an alternative minimum tax for businesses that pay little Federal Income Tax because of large credits or deductions.

President Obama talks about taking tax credits and deductions away from the rich oil companies, but he fails to acknowledge the historic change in natural gas and oil production which resulted from early high risk investments in fracking technology which reversed the long term decline in domestic gas and oil production. The financing of small wildcatters who helped spur the improvement in fracking technology was aided by the available tax credits.

Congress should consider adopting an income tax credit for employers for the first year of a cash wage increase of up to 5% (including a cash bonus) to an employee who is not included in the top 10% of the company's wage earners. They will have to consider rules to prevent gaming the system including requirements that head count or aggregate payroll to other employees not be decreased or the shifting of income between tax years.

In concluding a discussion on tax fairness, we should note how unfair it is to have sunset provisions in the tax laws and for the president and Congress to make it impossible for businesses and individuals to rationally plan their investment and spending decisions because of the tax uncertainties they cause.

ESTATE TAXATION

We have long had a Federal Estate Tax which taxes wealth after death and which under the American Taxpayer Relief Act of 2012 will remain in effect for estates above a $5,000,000 threshold or a family threshold of $10,000,000 ($5,000,000 for each spouse). The threshold is large enough to offer protection to most family businesses and farms. However, the tax rate was increased to 40% above the threshold.

The law as modified ends years of estate tax uncertainty and enables taxpayers to engage in long-term estate planning. Changes in the gift tax provisions make it easier and more tax advantageous to transfer property to children during one's lifetime.

The Estate Tax is an important source of revenue. It is the only tax levied on unrealized appreciation of assets (which has never been taxed except under the estate tax for valid reasons). It could have been enhanced and made a more important revenue source by limiting the use of dynasty trusts (as the King of England did by adopting the Rule Against Perpetuities long before the American Revolution) and by closing other loopholes available including the use of defective grantor trusts.

The Rule Against Estate Tax Avoidance

We should not permit our most successful businessmen to avoid paying taxes during their lifetime and at death. Rich individuals often create charitable foundations that continue in existence tax-free indefinitely and name their friends and issue (who often receive large fees) as managers. The capital appreciation of property of the type held by Bill Gates and Warren Buffett is never taxed if given to a charity or charitable foundation.

We should introduce The Rule Against Estate Tax Avoidance to limit charitable deductions for Federal Estate Tax purposes to one-half of a person's wealth and collect Federal Estate Tax on the remainder. We should do so in a way that does not significantly deter or interfere with charitable giving, which should remain fully deductible for federal income tax purposes.

If we added the aggregate of all charitable gifts made during a taxpayer's lifetime (the Aggregate Lifetime Charitable Gifts) back into the taxable estate (the Adjusted Taxable Estate) and then limited the charitable deduction for Federal Estate Tax purposes, which shall be calculated by adding the charitable gifts taking effect at death to the Aggregate Lifetime Charitable Gifts to one-half of the Adjusted Taxable Estate, the US Treasury will be able to collect a substantial tax (40% of 50%) from large estates to make up for not taxing unrealized appreciation during one's lifetime.

However, to prevent a taxpayer from giving away substantially more than what turns out to be one-half of his adjusted taxable estate prior to death and thereby become incapable of paying his Federal Estate Tax in full, taxpayers would have to disclose their Aggregate Lifetime Charitable Gifts on their Federal Income Tax returns and represent that the charitable gifts deducted for Federal Income Tax purposes in the current year will not reduce the current estimated value of taxpayer's remaining assets below the amount needed to pay the Federal Estate Tax if the taxpayer had died on the last day of the tax year. We might also recapture a portion of the last gifts given which reduce the value of the estate below the estate tax due.

For liquidity reasons we can permit an extended payment period of up to 10 years for the payment of Federal Estate taxes by illiquid estates. Alternatively, we can permit payment in kind by the delivery of certain qualifying assets. We might also permit a second alternative valuation date a few years after death to protect estates against declines in asset values during the extended payment period.

We might also require charitable foundations to distribute contributions received within a period of time such as 25 years after receipt.

ENTITLEMENTS

The word entitlements covers a broad range of federal government programs each of which has offered important societal benefits, including Social Security, Medicare, Medicaid, food stamps and other welfare programs to which we have now added Obamacare. They have in the aggregate created unsustainable federal obligations certain of which we must bring under control. The annual cost of providing entitlements is skyrocketing as the number of people reaching age 65 grows and life expectancy increases. Promoting a significant and sustained recovery will alleviate some of the entitlement strains by providing substantial additional tax revenues and reduce entitlement costs as a percentage of GDP. Slowing the growth of certain entitlements is not the equivalent of and should be distinguished from taking austerity measures that will cause job losses. The Great Recession and the inadequate recovery have limited GDP growth that in turn has magnified the burden of our growing entitlements.

Taxpayers contribute to the funding of certain of our entitlement such as Social Security and Medicare in the form of withholding taxes. Certain of our entitlements, which provide a safety net for families below the poverty level, including food stamps, Medicaid, free phones, transportation, housing subsidies and negative income taxes are made possible by American greatness. Long-term unemployment insurance benefits are becoming another entitlement as a result of our failure to create an adequate number of jobs.

The aggregate safety net payments exceed $30,000 per year for a family of four living in New York City not counting Medicaid payments, which total about $7,500 per person but are higher for the elderly. The laws under which safety net payments are calculated are extremely complex. They include a work requirement to prevent individuals from using the safety net as a lifetime benefit. Yet, the number of food stamp beneficiaries is growing rapidly. The cost of maintaining the safety net can be reduced if family members find good paying jobs that bring family incomes substantially above the poverty level. However, there has been a troubling development in recent years. A large number of potential workers seek part time or off-the-books employment so as not to lose or reduce their welfare benefits, which enables them to live reasonably comfortable lives. Since food stamp programs are adjusted for inflation and wages have stagnated, the problem is getting more serious over time.

We must remain diligent to provide good job opportunities and insure that welfare benefits are not so great that they discourage efforts to find better jobs. Unemployment benefits should be reduced and phased out over time so as to encourage meaningful efforts to find good paying jobs and end welfare dependency.

The aggregate number of Americans on food stamps exceeds 45 million, which seems suspiciously high. We can create a fairer society by undertaking a careful review of all safety net payments. We can reduce welfare benefits to millionaires who have little or no income because they are invested in cash and cheating by families or individuals claiming duplicate benefits for items such as food stamps or other claims for benefits to which they are not entitled. We created a negative income tax to encourage work. Now we must encourage welfare recipients to seek and accept better paying jobs.

Most politicians are afraid they will antagonize seniors if they even mention Social Security or Medicare reform. Senior citizens do not want to give up any of their benefits regardless of the cost to the government of providing them. Their only concern about the national debt is that they might lose some of their benefits. Representative Ryan's attempt to start a discussion on entitlement reform to apply only to individuals under age 55 opened the door for Democrat's to use scare tactics to frighten and gain votes from the elderly and soon to be retired. Workers under age 50 have serious doubts as to whether the Social Security and Medicare programs which they are contributing to will ever pay benefits to them. They are entitled to know what benefits they can expect to receive so that they can adopt their own long-term financial plans to meet their retirement needs.

President Obama has failed to propose a plan for dealing with our entitlement problems. On the contrary, he made our problems much worse by spearheading the adoption of Obamacare to get government involved with the providing of healthcare to all people under age 65. He did so at a time in our history when the growing national debt which ballooned because of the Great Recession and the failures of the Obama stimulus plans, require that both political parties work together in an effort to bring future entitlement payments under control. President Obama and other Democrats have waited for the Republicans to insist on dealing with entitlement modifications so that they can blame them for any changes that are made which reduce benefits.

Although disability payments are not generally considered as entitlements, fraudulent disability claims have become such a serious problem that they should be harshly dealt with as soon as possible.

SOCIAL SECURITY

Taking steps to bring long-term entitlements under control does not mean that we should ever consider reducing Social Security payments to those currently receiving benefits or who are within ten years of retirement. We must accept that as a "no-no" even if we have to print money to make the payments, which will lead to inflation. Social Security payments are designed to bear a relationship to contributions made over a lifetime of work. However, longevity has greatly increased the cost of providing benefits. The so-called Social Security Trust Fund is a myth. There is no separate fund. Social Security benefits are an obligation of the US Treasury. Because of longevity and the change in the ratio of beneficiaries to workers subject to Social Security withholding, the obligations for Social Security benefits in future years are going to substantially exceed Social Security withholding receipts.

The anticipated shortfall in Social Security funding has been met in the past by delaying the retirement age for the start of payments. We must make changes NOW similar to those made previously to adjust the age for the start of benefits for people under age 55 for longevity or change the way we adjust for inflation by modifying the cost of living formula. By changing Social Security rules, we can make it affordable based on actuarial statistics and guaranty its availability for the young workers who are currently contributing or at least reduce the short fall in collections needed to meet all obligations.

We should have made the needed changes years ago. The problem becomes worse as more people reach and approach retirement age. We are going to have to make larger adjustments or accept the fact that a larger portion of Social Security benefits will have to be paid out of tax revenues.

Not only has the Obama administration failed to deal with the Social Security problem, but, as part of its attempt to stimulate the economy, the Obama administration turned to "temporarily" reducing Social Security withholding taxes. To hide what it was doing to social security collections, Congress temporarily designated a portion of federal income tax receipts as Social Security withholding payments. The Obama administration's designation was an attempt to make it look like Social Security was still self-funded from the withholding tax payments and to avoid the argument that because people are making lesser contributions to Social Security they should get reduced benefits. We should try to maintain a relationship between Social Security contributions and benefits. Liberal Democrats may not care. Based upon their current practices they will merely suggest that we treat Social Security as an additional safety net payment.

President Obama has not proposed any further change to the age of commencement of benefits, which would adjust Social Security for longevity and slow Social Security funding needs but might have adverse political consequences. Instead, his actions have accelerated the need to make Social Security payments out of the Treasury. Unless we change the retirement age or the manner in which we calculate the adjustment for inflation or find a way to substantially grow the economy, meeting our Social Security obligations will require additional taxes (such as increasing the level of income subject to Social Security withholding tax) or reduced benefits for the rich, printing additional dollars or additional government borrowing. Treating rich people differently would represent a basic change in the concept of Social Security as being funded by one's own contributions. Nevertheless, both parties are already discussing means testing Social Security benefits. If you take away the benefits from the rich, their contributions become just another income tax.

We should not consider eliminating Social Security benefits for our younger workers and replacing them with individual accounts. Even if some people could do better investing their own retirement account, a significant percentage will lose money and need federal assistance. Everyone who has a job and is able to contribute to Social Security should have a predictable retirement check monthly regardless of their investment choices.

MEDICARE

Medicare is different. Medicare benefits are based on need and not equivalent to one's contributions. Some people's benefits greatly exceed the payments they have made into the system by a multiple of 20, 30, 40 or more for each dollar contributed. Medicare was broken before the adoption of Obamacare.

We know that as long as we permit the patient and his/her doctor to decide on healthcare needs with few limitations, future Medicare costs will increase by trillions of dollars as our population ages. We must find a way to deal with Medicare that honors our commitment to our senior citizens but is affordable by our government. We can make Medicare more cost-efficient but even then we will not be able to continue to offer our seniors unlimited high quality health care of the type they are currently receiving for more than a few years without increasing the national debt or printing very large amounts of money which will cause all the negative aspects of runaway inflation.

We adopted Medicare to fund and provide benefits for people of retirement age. Medicare payments are structured in a way that encourages doctors and other health care providers to order excessive treatments and procedures. Outcome is ignored. There are providers who game the system to obtain excessive payments, while others are underpaid.

Medicare costs are already out of control and will become more so in the future due in part to longevity. The age of eligibility should be delayed as we have done for Social Security. Furthermore, it is not realistic for beneficiaries to expect to receive unlimited health care benefits at no out-of-pocket cost particularly in the final years of their lives, which are ever being extended by improving but costly medical procedures and drugs. Although careful consideration has been given to limiting administrative costs, as well as to the method of compensating for the care provided without limiting the individual's choice in selecting and following the advice of the doctor of his or her choosing, costs will continue to grow uncontrollably.

We must consider instituting higher co-payments and deductibles for certain elective procedures to encourage each beneficiary to take good care of his or her health and not seek certain elective treatments or procedures. We might even provide a death benefit for those who limit discretionary treatments or procedures and have available unused benefits at death.

The failure to deal with theft from Medicare is a national disgrace. A "60 Minutes" program carefully detailed how multi-million dollar frauds are taking place but nothing gets done to stop it. Instead of budgeting sufficient funds to hire an expanded staff at the FBI to prevent Medicare theft and improve law enforcement, our politicians use the problem as a budgetary gimmick by claiming that they will reduce future Medicare costs by preventing theft in future years. We should provide for larger fines and mandatory long-term jail sentences for those who steal large amounts, such as $10 million or more, from Medicare.

MEDICAID

Government health care costs begin with Medicaid, the costs of which are paid in large part by the states to provide care for those who can't afford to pay. With such a large percentage of our population either unemployed or earning near or below the poverty level, Medicaid costs have skyrocketed and are contributing to the financial difficulties of many of our states. Obamacare greatly increases the cost of providing Medicaid. We must find ways to control Medicaid costs. Medicaid beneficiaries often use the local hospital emergency room as a substitute for a family doctor. Obamacare offers expanded insurance coverage that President Obama says will lower emergency room costs, but emergency rooms have to be available 24 hours a day in any event. Where is a parent going to find a doctor to treat their sick child at 3:00 AM except at an emergency room? We should consider using nurses rather than doctors during daytime hours to provide certain health care benefits to reduce costs.

While every person in the US should receive basic healthcare regardless of his or her ability to pay, Medicaid beneficiaries should not expect to receive the same level of discretionary care as individuals who pay for all or a significant portion of their health care coverage.

OBAMACARE

Obamacare entitled the "Affordable Care Act" creates a new entitlement that our country had no need to offer and is unable to afford. Like many Congressional laws the name is misleading. Pursuing Obamacare during the Great Recession was irresponsible. Medicaid, with more limited elective procedures than offered to people who pay for their insurance coverage, should remain the source of healthcare for the poor who need it. Businesses that were paying for most of the cost of healthcare for their employees and their families were finally beginning to get health care costs under control with co-pays and deductibles. Hospitals had been working with insurance companies to improve health care outcomes and reduce the cost of providing healthcare.

Congress has been unable to deal with the healthcare mess, which has been festering for years and which the Democrats rushed to exacerbate by adopting Obamacare. Now that it has been found to be Constitutional as a tax, we are going to discover its consequences unless it is modified or repealed, which is highly unlikely since President Obama has been reelected.

Obamacare is almost certain to cause a multi-trillion dollar increase in health care costs that will have to be paid for by individuals, businesses or taxpayers. The CBO has already recalculated the cost of Obamacare to show that it will exceed $1.75 trillion over 10 years. Obamacare also included a $700 billion reduction in Medicare funding, a tax for all who fail to purchase coverage, a .9% additional FICA tax, a 3.8% Medicare Contribution Tax, the latter unfairly targeted to married couples with income over $250,000 (and individuals with incomes over $200,000) and substantial investment income and a tax on medical equipment and drug manufacturers.

We must not forget that Obamacare was passed at a time when President Obama probably thought based upon bad advice, that his stimulus plan would lead to a quick turnaround in the economy and possibly didn't realize how unaffordable Obamacare would be. On the other hand, he may have thought that if he promised health care coverage to a large number of people and claimed it could be offered at no additional cost, it would gain votes for his reelection efforts regardless of the fact that the promise made no economic sense. A country that is about to engage in a costly expansion of subsidized health care should do so during a period of prosperity.

President Obama sought to offer benefits to further his socialist views. He seems to think that he can pay for medical care and his other welfare programs by raising the taxes on or confiscating the wealth of the people he calls rich and by taxing the providers of medical products and services that over time will pass the tax along through price increases. The new taxes imposed to partly fund Obamacare costs are the first step in the wrong direction. What most people fail to realize is that the Obamacare tax on individuals is really a second income tax. It is predictable that Democrats will seek other tax increases to pay for the cost of Obamacare.

We are eventually going to realize that the only way under Obamacare for our government to restrain the increase in the cost of purchasing insurance will be to reduce or deny payments to health care providers or benefits to selected beneficiaries. We cannot have unlimited health care at the election of the individual, but there are better ways to limit expenses than to give control of benefits to our inefficient and politically motivated federal government.

Prior to Obamacare being passed by Congress, the federal government provided healthcare for our senior citizens through Medicare and the states provided healthcare to the poor of all ages principally through Medicaid, which is in large part reimbursed by the federal government. Emergency rooms at hospitals are required to provide health care to anyone who seeks it whether or not they pay, with much of the unpaid amount being added to bills of others (including insurance providers who pass on their cost to their customers) able to pay. Obamacare confusingly attempts to change the method of providing coverage for healthcare including the promotion of health insurance exchanges that half of the states do not want to become involved with.

We have known for years that Medicare and Medicaid in the form currently offered and financed are too costly and unsustainable for more than a few more years unless we squeeze the healthcare providers financially as the population ages and costs for new treatments and procedures rise. The states, which must balance their budgets, are finding it impossible to meet Medicaid costs without cutting spending in other areas such as infrastructure spending, contributing to lost jobs and a deteriorating infrastructure nationwide.

To date we have been trying to control costs by limiting payments to doctors, many of whom have decided not to accept Medicare payments for their services. Many doctors have left the profession or elected to become hospital employees at reduced salaries because of the limits on their fees and soaring data collection, billing and malpractice insurance problems and costs. Obamacare will speed up the exodus of doctors whose education over many years is very expensive and whose salaries pale as compared to corporate executives, investment banking employees and money managers. It is going to be more difficult for medical schools to attract the top students.

Adding 30 million new healthcare beneficiaries and disregarding pre-existing conditions are generous gestures included in Obamacare but the extra costs will have to be paid for. Our entitlement programs will ultimately have to offer reduced or less timely services or be paid for by charging higher fees, further taxing the rich, overcharging young people, and taxing medical equipment and drug suppliers (who will try to pass the costs on to customers) or by borrowing or printing dollars, which will lead to high rates of interest and inflation.

Prior to Obamacare, the double digit increases in the cost of providing healthcare for people under age 65, which has fallen in large part on employers, has been a major business and individual problem for many years. Over time health care insurance has become less catastrophic insurance coverage and more an excessively costly system for allocating and paying for rapidly growing treatments and procedures, which everyone would like their family members to receive with no or minimum out-of-pocket payment. As new treatments become available, it is imperative that we find a better way to allocate the benefits that we should supply to individuals without their having to pay for all or a significant portion of the cost. In recent years, prior to the adoption of Obamacare, insurance providers have attempted to meet the demands of business to contain health care costs by limiting covered procedures and enlarging deductibles and co-pays.

Even though Obamacare is unpopular President Obama used certain benefits provided by it as election issues. He called attention to the benefits it provides for college age children, the coverage for 30 million additional Americans, the elimination of pre-existing conditions as grounds to deny coverage, and the personal savings from the elimination of the doughnut hole for prescription drug plan coverage. However, he ignored the costs of providing such additional benefits. Increasing the age for inclusion of children under a family plan is favored by a large percentage of the population. It is a benefit that adds only a small cost for each family with coverage and Governor Romney and most voters, favored it. On the other hand, the cost of providing coverage to 30 million additional people, many of whom have preexisting conditions, can be expected to cost trillions of dollars more than current estimates. Many young individuals who are being greatly overcharged under Obamacare will opt out and pay the penalty, which is small.

They can buy insurance when and if they need it without worrying about pre-existing conditions.

Allowing healthy people to pay a small tax to avoid paying for healthcare coverage they do not presently need but which will be available to them at the same cost if they become ill is not a prudent way to run a healthcare insurance business. Look for the penalty to rise in future years.

President Obama proudly tells millions of seniors that he has saved them thousands of dollars by eliminating the doughnut hole from prescription drug coverage. The doughnut hole was designed to keep costs down by discouraging unnecessary drug usage and encouraging the use of less costly generic drugs over prescription drugs. The Democrats hid the cost of elimination of the doughnut hole by inducing prescription drug suppliers to temporarily reduce their prices and by charging a tax beginning in 2013 on drug suppliers. However, facing reduced profitability, drug manufacturers have reduced their R&D expenditures; unless they get a fair return, future development of new drugs will be impeded.

We must attempt to bring health care costs under control for people under age 65 without reducing the availability or quality of care. Except to the extent that our federal government contributes to the providing of healthcare to the poor through Medicaid, it did not have to get involved. Private industry was working on solving the problem.

Obamacare was passed based on deliberately misleading revenue and cost estimates designed to make it look cost effective. Certain fraudulent claims were exposed as such even before most of the provisions became effective. For example, it offered long-term care coverage designed to make it look like Obamacare would be revenue positive in the initial years.

Long-term care insurance is sold based on the expectation that policy holders will pay in premiums over a period of many years before a limited number of them become so incapacitated as to qualify for large daily benefits. Insurers selling long-term care policies set aside reserves to pay for the inevitable very substantial benefits to a limited number of beneficiaries in later years. The negative aspects of the long-term care provisions, which over time would have cost taxpayers trillions of dollars, were exposed and the long-term care provisions were repealed shortly after Obamacare was passed and before any long term care policies were offered for sale (but not until after it was passed based on misleading revenue projections).

Americans must be encouraged to improve their health through diet, exercise and personal care. However, even if people live longer, healthier lives they will eventually have to face age-related health problems. We must also use co-pays and deductibles and life-time limits for elective medical services and procedures to encourage patients and their doctors to be selective and cost conscious in their health care usage. It is clear that President Obama and the liberal Democrats want to lead us to socialized medicine from birth to grave, which, to manage cost, will inevitably result in a reduction in the quality and availability of medical care except for those people willing and able to pay for their own care. Unless modified, Obamacare will inevitably lead to a system where healthcare allocation will become controlled by the government and rationed under a politically controlled system except for those who pay their own way using doctors who elect not to accept Medicare or Medicaid patients.

The confusion caused by Obamacare and businesses' fear of healthcare cost increases has impeded the economic recovery. Some small businesses seeking to be exempt from Obamacare requirements, which apply to businesses with 50 or more employees, are not hiring full time workers and others are laying off workers. Businesses seeking to increase profitability are looking at opportunities presented by Obamacare to avoid having to continue to supply heath care by paying a small penalty. Even if they give wage increases in lieu of providing health care coverage their employees are going to have to pay for health care with after-tax dollars unless Congress changes the tax laws.

President Obama should acknowledge the deficiencies of Obamacare that have become apparent in the period since its adoption and meet with representative of both parties to attempt to modify or eliminate the most egregious provisions to improve health care outcomes and reduce costs.

Everyone needs healthcare at some time, and quality care is expensive to provide. We must find a way of providing health care that is of the highest quality within affordable limits and lets doctors earn a deserved rate of income for practicing medicine to the best of their ability. That can only happen when (i) we recognize that we cannot afford to provide Medicare and Medicaid beneficiaries whatever medical services the patient and his/her doctor wants for free and we must have significant deductibles, copays or lifetime limits, (ii) we greatly improve the method in which doctors are paid including simplifying required forms, (iii) we recognize that doctors are human and will make mistakes and find ways to help those patients affected, but put strict limits on tort liability, (iv) we create a less expensive system utilizing trained technicians or nurses to provide basic childcare such as giving vaccinations and treating the regular childhood diseases.

OUT OF CONTROL BANKS

The banking industry is out of control.

The banking industry has evolved over the past 50 years to a sad state in which too few banks follow sound banking practices. Our bankers have changed the way they treat customers. It was not incompetent credit verification that led banks to offer home mortgages and credit cards with excessive limits to people who are poor credit risks. Bankers gave mortgages with teaser loan rates to borrowers they knew had poor credit expecting to sell the mortgages to FNMA and Freddie Mac or third party investors or package and sell them as MBSes. They expected the holder of the mortgage to profit from resetting interest rates and prepayment penalties when the mortgages were refinanced. They knew that the refinanced mortgages were in increased principal amounts and the borrowers were not developing or were reducing the equity in their homes. It was inevitable that when housing prices stopped going up many of the borrowers would have to default.

The banks concurrently developed a system that deliberately gives credit to poor credit risk individuals. They know that they will have a high level of default from such high-risk borrowers. To make a profit, they charge exorbitant interest rates to cardholders who don't pay their full balance on time and late fees to those holders who fail to pay the minimum balance a short time after receipt of the monthly statement. These excessive interest rates and late fees are paid in large part by the working poor and middle class cardholders, many of whom are forced to use up their savings to make the required payments. Such payments enable banks to recover their bad debts and make profits from the credit card advances.

The banks go to extraordinary efforts to get cardholders to pay loan shark interest rates. They send confusing statements requiring minimum payments but designed to encourage or trick the holder into paying only a portion of the total leaving a high interest rate balance. They from time to time send enticing blank checks to encourage the cardholder to create high interest debt immediately upon use. If you use a check in an emergency and can't pay the next bill in full, you may become trapped into becoming a high interest debtor. They also locate their billing and collection offices in a state where the invoice or payment might have a delivery delay so that payment by the unwary will be received a day or two late and subject to late fees and interest charges, which will appear on the next statement. What is happening effectively is that those people who by accident or design fail to pay their credit cards on time but who are able to pay the high interest charges and late fees over time wind up paying for the non-credit worthy borrowers who fail to pay.

We want to give low income families access to the banking system, but the use of debit cards which are prefunded and do not entail cash outlays by the banks rather than credit cards is the better way to give them such access. Debit cards are already available to food stamp recipients. The small extra cost, if any, can be passed on in overall debit and credit card charges.

Years ago the banks used their lobbyists to convince Congress to change the bankruptcy laws to make it more difficult for borrowers to avoid credit card liabilities by going bankrupt, but the banks can't always collect the balances due. The banks justify their incorrigible interest rates by pointing out their facilitation of consumer purchases by extending credit to high-risk cardholders. So do other loan sharks. We should note that even their outrageous tactics did not prevent the banks from taking credit card losses during the Great Recession. Think of the damage they did to the borrowers and our economy. Free market capitalism needs to be regulated with usury laws that prevent lenders from gouging individual borrowers.

We don't need thousands of pages of legislation to correct one of the most egregious bank practices. We can adopt a national usury law providing in one sentence that no lender may charge an interest rate in excess of (i) 5 or 6% or (ii) 2 or 3% above the 10 year US Treasury note rate on any loan to an individual having a term of less than 5 years. We might consider phasing in the usury law over a 3-5 year period. Of course we will need regulations to prevent lenders from avoiding the law.

It will be argued that usury laws will reduce consumer spending and be detrimental to the economy. It is true that if bank interest rates are subject to a usury law banks will restrict credit to high-risk individuals who may be prevented from making purchases they can't afford except for cash or on a debit card. On the other hand, the reduced interest charges to people who use credit cards and the interest and penalties saved by those people denied credit cards will make more money available to them to spend.

We should also apply usury laws to the check cashing entities that rip off the poor who do not have access to the banking system.

The principal beneficiaries of bank operations in the past ten years have been the bank executives many of whom benefitted from fraudulent financial statements and short sellers who took advantage of the banking collapse. Bank executives have little personal investment and are managing other people's money. The compensation packages negotiated with friendly boards of directors promoted excessive risk taking. If management was successful, both management and shareholders would benefit. If they failed and suffered losses the shareholders, bondholders and the US government, which must prevent the collapse of the system, became the losers. Often, especially when questionable or fraudulent accounting practices were used, the failure was not discovered until after management executives had realized enormous profits. One of the great government failures of the latest banking collapse has been the failure to bring civil and criminal prosecutions against many of the wrongdoers or even make a valid attempt to recover the ill-begotten gains.

Some people blame the deregulation of the banks and the low interest rate policies generated by actions of the Fed for the housing, mortgage and banking bubbles. The ability of banks to pursue business opportunities subject to limited regulations and to obtain capital at low interest rates should have enabled them to make sound investments and offer mortgages and credit card loans at reasonable interest rates to benefit consumers and businesses and increase the banks' profitability. It is no excuse for the reckless and greedy actions of our bankers, many of whom got rich by negligently or fraudulently reporting falsified profits from the issuance of unsound mortgages and MBSes and the investment in high risk securities and derivatives, which ultimately led to the insolvency of their employers.

We had adequate laws and regulations in place. The Fed or other bank regulatory agencies should have prevented unsound lending practices. Despite the poor quality of the mortgages placed in MBSes, almost all MBSes were AAA rated by the major rating agencies. The fraudulent or grossly negligent ratings purchased for a fee from conflicted ratings companies facilitated the worldwide sales of hundreds of billions of dollars of MBSes to investors as highly rated, low risk securities. The

MBS underwriter's insatiable need for mortgages to be placed in MBSes regardless of quality led to the offering of no-down-payment, teaser rate and no-document mortgages. In some cases, the mortgages were granted based on fraudulent loan applications. Mortgage brokers helped borrowers fraudulently modify applications so that the mortgage would be granted. No one cared.

Many MBSes owning junk mortgages eventually proved to be almost worthless, precipitating the banking collapse and hundreds of billions of dollars of investment losses by pension plans and other retirement accounts. MBSes, with their different tranches and complex documentation, have created a creditor's rights and foreclosure priority mess. After the collapse often highly leveraged investors who bought MBSes with money borrowed from banks defaulted and the MBSes being held as collateral were transferred to the banks. Some holders of MBS securities have brought successful fraud actions to rescind their purchases or recover damages.

The Securities Act of 1933, as amended, has been in place for over 75 years to prevent the fraudulent sale of securities. Its definition of fraud includes a failure to state a material fact. At some point of time when mortgages included in MBSes began defaulting in large numbers selling junk bonds as AAA securities was clearly fraudulent. The fact that bankers claimed reliance on AAA ratings they knew to be false is not a defense to a fraud action. The SEC wasn't paying attention while the sales were taking place. It was also derelict in failing to review the financial statements of banks and investment banks after the collapse of the MBS market in order to identify the entities that overstated profits to justify paying excessive bonuses to executives by using fraudulent accounting practices and failing to create adequate reserves for losses during the credit bubble and after it collapsed. While bankers are entitled to use reasonable discretion in establishing reserves, a clear abuse of discretion by failing to create adequate reserves for income accounting purposes is a violation of the Securities Act of 1934. When the mortgage and banking bubbles burst, many of our major banks had liabilities exceeding the fair value of their assets, many of which were in the form of claims against insolvent third parties or were illiquid.

Many banks facing large losses were fraudulently reporting profits even after the housing market began to decline and mortgage payments were in default. Rather than declaring mortgages to be in default for non-payment, they restructured them to add the un-made payments to the principal and reported profits by treating the mortgages as if the payments had been made. During the Great Recession, regulators, in an attempt to help banks survive, permitted the banks to get away with hiding their losses by changing the accounting rules and allowing them to carry MBSes at cost rather than fair market value, but that did not excuse appropriate footnote disclosures.

We learn about the merits and failures of the hastily passed, multi-thousand page Dodd-Frank law one issue at a time. Many of the provisions and regulations of Dodd-Frank are still being interpreted and many of the required regulations are still being written.

Dodd-Frank's numerous titles covering a broad range of activities a) create the Financial Stability Oversight Council to deal with financial stability and promote market discipline and establish the Office of Financial Research to gather data and report to the Council and other Government agencies, b) provide for orderly liquidation authority, c) transfer additional power to the Comptroller of the Currency, the FDIC and the Fed, d) provide for regulation of investment advisors, e) establish a Federal Insurance Office, f) adopt the Volcker Rule, g) provide for regulation of swaps and derivatives, h) give the Fed an additional role in the supervision of risk management, i) authorize the SEC to impose regulations for investor protection, provide payment for whistleblowers, improve regulation of credit rating agencies, improve the asset backed securities process and authorize meaningless shareholder approvals of executive compensation, j) create a Bureau of Consumer Financial Protection to regulate consumer financial products and services, k) create new standards for the Fed, l) provide incentives for low income people to gain access to mainstream financial institutions, m) limit the reuse of TARP funds and n) provide for mortgage reforms.

It is difficult to understand why Congress created the Financial Stability Oversight Council. Maybe the Democratic controlled Congress thought that one more agency would accomplish what the existing agencies were failing to do.

Dodd-Frank has some useful provisions that attempt to deal with a number of problems created by bankers that were previously not being regulated, but it was passed as a work-in-progress. It has caused confusion and billions of dollars of annual compliance costs with limited benefit. It places too much emphasis on banning proprietary trading by banks, which was not the cause of the Great Recession. The Dodd-Frank banking bill was drafted by many of the same people who had helped encourage the housing and banking excesses. Maybe that is why the Dodd-Frank legislation does not prevent the low down payment loans to poor credit risks that contributed to the housing and banking collapse.

The repeal of the Glass-Steagall Act years before the collapse of Lehman Brothers opened the door for banks to go into investment banking, led to the creation of many trillions of derivative securities, the risks of which even the originators often failed to understand, and the use of excessive leverage by banks to purchase high-risk investments. The Volker Rule is in effect an attempt to re-adopt the main concept of the Glass-Steagall Act and separate traditional banking from bank's proprietary trading, which is severely limited.

For months, the large international banks and their lobbyists have been objecting to the effects of making the Volker Rule operative. The drafters of Dodd-Frank did look at the various business functions performed by our international banks and exempted the hedging transactions of banks to facilitate the transactions of their clients. However, because the banks are hedging for their own and not their client's account they are at risk. Once the bank has a hedge in place it can be sold or further hedged in the same manner as any proprietary risk purchase. Since clients can buy or sell almost anything, the banks' hedging practices should and will be permitted to cover a very broad spectrum of loans, securities and derivatives.

Dodd-Frank does make a valid attempt to deal with derivative securities. We read about the many trillions of dollars of derivative securities that were previously to a large extent unregulated. We must better regulate derivatives by requiring greater collateral thereby reducing counter party risk. Recent rules adopted by exchanges making derivatives more uniform and requiring additional collateral is a good first step, but we need regulators who are capable of understanding the risks associated with complex derivative securities.

We must undertake a definitive study of derivative securities, and credit default swaps in particular. When you issue a credit default swap, you are betting against a default. We should carefully consider banning the sale of credit default swaps, which have a risk of loss of 100% if you are on the wrong side of the bet. The seller of a credit default swap often receives a token payment for what it erroneously believes is a small risk and then such seller itself becomes a third party risk as the exposure, which it had no reliable way to assess (such as the risk of a sovereign government bond default), develops into a major risk over time. There is something inherently wrong with betting on the failure of a company or a country to pay its bonds and then using everything in your power to cause the failure to occur.

The argument that credit default swaps allow borrowers to pay lesser interest rates is specious. It only applies if a fool underprices the risk of selling a credit default swap. If credit default swaps are properly priced, their cost offsets the interest rate savings. One is not allowed to purchase fire insurance on his neighbor's home. Even if we limit the size of the loss on a credit default swap and we require 100% collateralization from both parties (in other words, both parties deposit the amount of the bet in cash), because of leverage (i.e., using borrowed money to collateralize the risk) the loss might jeopardize the loser's ability to pay its other debts thereby creating systemic risk. The banks argue that their substantial equity serves as collateral for all of their risks. However, a substantial equity didn't help Lehman Brothers when its illiquid assets suddenly declined in value and customers withdrew funds.

Many Americans who do not understand the negative effect that a collapse of the banking system would have on business and their personal lives opposed TARP. They insist that our government eliminate too-big-to-fail considerations in the event of a future banking crisis. They do not understand that while TARP and the Fed's actions have saved many banks from failure, stockholders and bondholders of some of the largest and worst run banks have lost over 90% or all of their equity value.

Arguments to the effect that in a capitalistic system if you make a bad investment you should lose your money, go bankrupt and go out of business shouldn't be applied to our banks. If our banking system collapses, our entire economy will be put into jeopardy. We have learned from the collapse of Lehman Brothers and other banks and investment banks shortly thereafter that the US Government must step in to maintain the solvency of the banking system. We can demagogue about too big to fail but our government has to be prepared to save the banking system the next time it is in jeopardy. Even if we split our large banks into smaller banks, failure of a large number of medium-size banks would still risk unacceptable systemic failure. We learned from the TARP program that by providing short term liquidity the US Government can prevent a collapse of the system and recover most if not all of the funding over time by the Fed's use of QE to make the banks profitable.

We must recognize that free market capitalism has led to the use of excessive leverage and the investment in excessively risky investments by banks controlled by executives who are greatly overcompensated for success but do not share in losses. We must regulate leverage and restrict risk-taking by banks. We must regulate banks so that failure of large banks is the exception rather than an every 6-12 month event.

A bank making low-risk mortgage loans requiring a 20% down payment on a carefully appraised home has become an unusual event. We must find a way to get regional banks to take the lead in restoring the practice.

Our large international banks seek risky investments because of the higher profit potential. Like bad gamblers, they often see only the upside and underestimate the downside risks. The combination of using high leverage and purchasing high-risk assets is a recipe for disaster. Dodd-Frank attempts to limit bank leverage to 15-1, but that amount is clearly excessive if the bank is going to speculate aggressively by buying or shorting high risk assets.

To better understand the risk associated with excess leverage we can compare the use of 15-1 leverage with 1-1 leverage permitted when buying securities on margin. When investing on 1-1 margin leverage with a 25% maintenance requirement, if you buy $1000 worth of a security and borrow $500 you get a margin call if the value of the security declines to $667 or by about 1/3. If a bank buys $1.6 million dollars of assets at 15-1 leverage it puts up $100,000 and borrows $1,500,000. Its equity is wiped out if the investment declines below $1,500,000 in value. It is no surprise that banks and investment banks with hundreds of billions of dollars of assets get wiped out when their asset base, particularly if not diversified and invested in high-risk assets, declines in value by 7% or more. During the past 5 years a large percentage of investments in subprime home mortgages and sovereign debt (even if believed to be hedged) held by banks and other entities leveraged at more than 15-1 declined in value by substantially more than that percentage.

Now a few years after the Lehman Brothers collapse, most banks claim they have strong balance sheets and have returned to profitability using a variety of accounting gimmicks that rely on rules allowing the banks to under-reserve their mortgage-related losses. They have reaped large profits from the virtually interest-free money loaned to them by the Fed, a large portion of which they invested at a profit in longer term US government debt, which paid a higher rate of interest and increased in value as interest rates declined. However, many of our largest banks remain undercapitalized for the highly leveraged risks they take.

Regulators are currently debating the interpretation of the restriction on proprietary trading by banks as contrasted to permissible hedging transactions to facilitate client activity, which may promote important business transactions. It's an exercise in futility. The banks will claim that every risk trade they make is a hedging transaction. We have learned from the publicized JP Morgan Chase trading loss, which they claim was a hedging transaction that hedging transactions may present risks similar to those associated with proprietary trading. We can expect that our unscrupulous bankers in their thirst to make high-risk investments will encourage clients to take positions so that the banks can hedge against them.

Nevertheless, it is not the right time to suddenly invoke the Volker Rule. The Great Recession was not caused by investment banking or proprietary trading but by bad lending practices and excessive leveraging of high-risk portfolios. The Volker rule is going to be almost impossible to enforce without curtailing important client transactions. Moreover, investment banking and proprietary trading has become ingrained in the business and investment portfolios of banks, and eliminating them will remove a potential income stream and result in significant job losses.

Proprietary trading is not the problem. Excess leverage coupled with overly aggressive risk taking is the problem. Investing in one or two large risk positions representing only a small percentage of a bank's capital does not put a bank in jeopardy because well-capitalized banks can absorb isolated large losses. However, the systemic risk to the monetary system changes when a large number of highly leveraged banks invest a high multiple of their capital in similar high-risk investments. Such positions become difficult to liquidate because taken as a whole they represent large positions. Large positions by reason of their size create a liquidity hazard because it takes time to get out of the position (for the same reason it takes a full bathtub a long time to drain). The problem is exacerbated when other investors (including high speed traders using complex computer programs) learn that a bank is trying to liquidate a position and can sell short, looking to cover at a lower price as the bank completes it liquidation of the security. In today's financial world, a bank's disclosing its serious problems makes them worse and the Federal Securities laws require such disclosure.

Our bankers still believe they can make large profits from highly leveraged, high-risk positions. Maybe they can. The problem is that the potential failure of a large bank or a number of smaller banks would create a systemic risk to the banking system, as occurred after the collapse of the housing, mortgage and banking bubbles, and we have no choice but to prevent them from failing. If they are successful, they keep their profits (which they can use to take even larger risk positions and pay bonuses to executives, dividends and repurchase shares of their stock) but if they incur large losses and become insolvent, the stockholders and bondholders lose most or all of their investment and the excess of such losses have to be absorbed by third parties or the taxpayers. Management retires to live on their excess compensation or fraudulently obtained profits or move on to other opportunities to invest other people's money.

Our over-leveraged banks own hundreds of billions of dollars in proprietary or hedged positions. It is very difficult for banks to assess risk. Because market conditions can change almost instantly and often do so whenever markets are under severe stress, a holder never can be sure whether it will be difficult to sell a large position or even a number of small positions concentrated in the same types of assets or to unwind what is thought was a conservative investment or a carefully hedged position. To liquidate a hedged position, you must liquidate both sides simultaneously or you wind up with a long or short position. It is often more difficult because of market conditions to close out one side of a position than the other. It seems that every few months we hear about an entity sustaining a large unexpected loss from what was thought to be a well-hedged position.

We have carried out stress tests on our banks and investment banks and given passing marks to almost all of the banks. There is no need to look at the stress tests to know that they are most likely flawed. Bank regulators must constantly assess each bank's risk profile and leverage to prevent history from repeating itself. In order to do so, our regulators must have personnel capable of assessing the risk of loss of the bank's investments. Depending on the investment portfolio, a bank may be overleveraged at 10-1 or less. Many of our bank executives are either eternal optimists or willing to risk all of the bank's capital by excessive risk taking seeking to earn large bonuses if they succeed. They may not be accounting properly for the risk that attaches to the forced liquidation of assets (particularly large positions) during a stressful period.

Banks that invest in high-risk assets should be required to significantly reduce their leverage. No highly leveraged bank should be permitted to reduce its capital by paying more than a token dividend or to repurchase shares, which reduces equity capital and increases leverage. Will our regulators ever learn from history? In recent years, too many of the banks we thought were adequately capitalized have become insolvent, filed bankruptcy, and gone out of business overnight.

In a stable economy with a revived housing market, banks should be able to earn a reasonable return on capital with leverage of less than 10-1.

We must remain diligent in detecting and avoiding what may turn out to be the next monetary problem. For example, questions have been raised as to whether money market funds or the government should guaranty the $1 price. For many years, most money market fund investors were looking for a way to get a return not available from their checking account without risking the principal and have their money conveniently available when needed. Now that short-term government interest rates are virtually nonexistent, they are generally not looking for a return but merely the protection of their capital. Greedy money market managers are willing to take risks with the principal in order to try to generate sufficient interest to pay their management fees. If the US Government is not willing to guarantee these investments against loss, we should either prevent money market funds from taking these types of risk or make it crystal clear in every statement to their customers that the government will not guaranty the $1 principal. Investors who want protection should be investing in FDIC insured deposits. If we want to preserve money market funds, which provide liquidity to the business community, we must either provide a US government guaranty or find a way to share the risk of loss so that a run on the fund does not benefit the first investors out and leave the loss to the remaining investors.

ROLE OF THE SEC, CFTC AND FINANCIAL STABILITY OVERSIGHT COUNCIL

Prior to the turn of the century, most Americans believed that the SEC acted as a watchdog to protect investors. It was generally believed that on occasion the SEC missed some wrongdoing that should have been discovered. The SEC over the years has evolved from being a highly qualified protector of public investors to an inadequately staffed governmental agency relying on the large accounting firms to create the rules for regulating and to oversee the financial disclosures made by publicly owned entities. The SEC staff is overwhelmed by the enormity of the task and fails to detect most securities frauds until long after investors have suffered losses. They also seem to be incapable of understanding and preventing various manipulative practices availed of by short term traders. The SEC requires hundreds of additional employees capable of regulating financial disclosures and understanding and regulating securities trading practices. Hiring such additional staff should be cost effective based on the filing fees and fines it collects.

Accounting firms for their own preservation have carefully attempted to avoid responsibility and potential liability for their client's financial statements. The accounting profession has been instrumental in developing the principle that the financial statements have been prepared by and are the responsibility of the company and not the accountants who merely issue a report. In the report, they advise the reader that their responsibility is to express an opinion on the company's internal control over financial reporting based on their audit, which is conducted in accordance with the standards of the Public Accounting Oversight Board (United States).

The auditors state in a typical report: "Those standards require that we plan and perform the audit to obtain reasonable assurance about whether effective internal control over financial reporting was maintained in all material respects. Our audit included obtaining an understanding of internal control over financial reporting, assessing the risk that a material weakness exists, testing and evaluating the design and operating effectiveness of internal control based on the assessed risk, and performing such other procedures as we considered necessary in the circumstances. We believe that our audit provides a reasonable basis for our opinion." They might go on to add language such as: "Because of the inherent limitation of internal controls over financial reporting, including the possibility of collusion or improper override of management of controls, material misstatements due to error or fraud may not be prevented or detected on a timely basis." In other words, the auditors are telling you that they review and opine on the internal accounting controls, but basically accept the company's numbers.

After the turn of the century, our bankers, and investment bankers created many trillions of dollars of credit default swaps and many other derivatives, which should have been treated as securities and carefully regulated by the SEC even before the adoption of the Dodd-Frank legislation.

Now our bankers and investment bankers armed with highly qualified legal teams, lobbyists and investment experts are trying to carve out exceptions from many of the Dodd-Frank provisions directed at reducing risk-taking by our banks and investment banks. Congress and the regulators are trying to interpret or modify Dodd-Frank to prevent a future financial collapse without overly restricting banking activity or impeding the economic recovery. It will be years before we know whether Dodd-Frank and its added rules and regulations and compliance costs have strengthened or weakened our financial system.

DEFENSE SPEENDING AND HOMELAND SECURITY

We must remain the world's foremost military power. We must be prepared at all times to defend our homeland and our allies. Although it seems to have been forgotten by too many Americans, we fought the wars in Iraq and Afghanistan after 9/11/2001 to retaliate against and restrain terrorists. Misleading statements may have been made about Iraq having weapons of mass destruction, but they were irrelevant. Saddam Hussein was supporting terrorists. Americans look at the imperfect nations being formed in Iraq and Afghanistan and question the purpose and success of those wars. We will never be able to evaluate the importance of those wars in avoiding terrorist acts within the US after 9/11/2001.

Many Americans are war weary and because President Obama and the liberal press have engendered a false sense of security based on claims that Al Qaeda is on the run they seem unconcerned about the risks of leaving Iraq and Afghanistan too early or terrorist threats around the world. We seem overly anxious to bring our troops home and run the risk that we will be allowing terrorists to regroup and take control of Iraq and Afghanistan and other Middle Eastern and African countries.

In order for us to protect our homeland, we must be ready to deal firmly with hostile leadership in countries that have or develop nuclear or other weapons of mass destruction, or such weapons may become available to terrorist organizations anywhere in the world. Financial sanctions never seem to be sufficient to prevent weapons development. Suicide bombers and simplified missile delivery capability controllable remotely by cell phones make the world an ever more dangerous place. Each year the potential for the murder of millions of people by terrorists increases. We must be more vigilant and enhance our ability to prevent that from happening.

We must develop a shield to protect our homeland, our overseas bases and our embassies against missile attacks similar to the one used by Israel to defend itself from missiles fired by Hamas. It is hard to believe that we assisted in the shield when it was being developed by Israel but have failed to design and build one of our own even if it offers only limited protection. We must also greatly increase the size of the Coast Guard to prevent against missiles being launched from small boats off our shores.

It is too early to tell whether the "Arab Spring" is going to lead to friendly or dangerous anti-American Muslim-controlled governments.

An increasing number of terrorist cells are operating throughout the world. We must adopt policies similar to those followed by Israel to retaliate against terrorist acts originating within a country by bombing the areas from which the terrorist attack was launched and killing the terrorists determined to be responsible even if the country denies its involvement. It is clear that we are currently doing so in or use of drones in Yemen and Pakistan.

Israel, faced with the treat of a nuclear attack from Iran, has made it clear that it will not ignore history and has indicated it is preparing to take preventive action if Iran passes what Israel determines to be a red line in its development of a nuclear weapon. President Obama who clearly did not want anything to happen before the election has created serious doubt as to whether he will authorize our military to provide assistance to Israel if it does so. Nor is it clear that the US will stand behind its commitments to Israel if attacked by any of its neighbors or if it takes preventive or retaliatory actions against them. He has time and again during his presidency demeaned the Israeli Government.

Harry Truman authorized the use of an A-bomb to speed the end of World War II. There is a question as to whether the Israeli Government faced with a threat of extinction would authorize a preventive or retaliatory nuclear strike to safeguard Israel or what the consequences might be. It is doubtful that President Obama, despite his strong words to the Iranian government, would ever launch a preventive strike of any kind to protect our country or an ally.

President Obama seeks to finance his socialist programs and the economic recovery by reducing defense expenditures. Some of his military advisers argue that in the changing military environment certain military equipment is no longer effective and shouldn't be maintained or replaced. We may never know why our government declined to provide military support requested by our embassy personnel in Libya. Possibly it resulted from a presidential determination to reduce our military expenditures and to rely on a weak local government to protect our embassy. The failure to protect our embassy personnel and apparent attempt to hide the truth from the American people by spreading a false explanation is difficult to understand.

Homeland security, which is dependent in large part upon on military strength, must remain our number one priority. It is essential for our president to maintain our status as the world's only superpower (which is going to last only until China equals or exceeds the US as a military superpower). The leaders of our country must recognize that (i) maintaining or increasing the amount of military expenditures to develop advanced weaponry is necessary for our long term security, (ii) that defense spending represents a major source of US based jobs, and (iii) that sale of armaments to allies are a major US revenue source that helps reduce the federal deficit and improves our international payments accounts while strengthening our allies ability to defend themselves. Our politicians should be working together to ensure that sequestration, which is included in the Fiscal Cliff, is avoided and defense cuts are not made.

We should take the following actions, some in the near term and others over the next 25 years to upgrade homeland security:

1. For homeland security purposes, we must increase defense spending to develop antimissile defenses and other devices to be better prepared to prevent an attack on our homeland or our allies by rogue countries like Iran and North Korea or terrorist groups supplied by them. We must also expand our rapid response capability and procedures to counter attack and decimate the sources of such attacks.

2. Shortly after 9/11/2001 we should have required all US residents to obtain a US Identification Card. (US ID) to make it easier to identify and track potential home grown and foreign terrorists. It is time we did so. A USID can be used to identify future undocumented immigrants in connection with the adoption of a change in our immigration laws to permit undocumented immigrants currently in the US to be given status as legal residents and a path to citizenship.

3. Homeland security requires that we enlarge our homeland security force to better control our borders and ports of entry to prevent entry of terrorists and weapons of mass destruction. Returning veterans are uniquely qualified for this purpose. Such force will also deter the entry of illegal immigrants and facilitate a change in our immigration laws.

4. We must expand the homeland security network to coordinate all of the current efforts to prevent domestic terrorism and to be ready to deal with the damage caused by all types of terrorist acts that may occur. Returning service personnel will be good candidates for this task.

5. We need an expanded joint military and space program to maintain our lead in space travel and communications satellites and to protect our satellites, the Internet and our wireless communication network from attack of any kind.

CHINA

During the past ten years China has become a major economic power and is growing at a pace to challenge the US before the end of the decade as the world's leading economic power. It has become dependent on the worldwide economy. Despite its communist background, there is no reason why China and the US cannot develop a relationship to work together to promote world peace and growth and improve living standards worldwide. China's behavior continues to be erratic. It has been rapidly expanding its military capability. Although it appears contrary to its economic interest it is involved with a dispute with Japan over certain uninhabited islands that is interfering with business dealings between the world's second and third largest economies. The Chinese who rely so heavily on exports should be more sensitive to boycotting imports.

It is easy for politicians to blame China and other countries for our jobs problem. Many of our manufacturing jobs migrated to China and other third world countries, but our consumers received the benefit of greatly reduced product prices that improved their standard of living. Many American entities profit from doing business in Asia.

As China develops its middle class it is growing its demand for our consumer products, machinery and equipment, autos and planes many of which are manufactured or serviced by US entities. Some of the lost middle class jobs were replaced by job growth at our exporters and international entities. China was not responsible for the most significant US job losses that resulted from the housing and banking collapse and the Great Recession that followed, and maintained and increased its dollar investments during the US downturn. Recent large investments by Chinese individuals in US real estate are generating price increases in many large US cities and helping to revive housing construction.

China and other developing nations need to create jobs for their large and restless populations. They have not developed adequate legal systems. They have until recently generally ignored harmful dumping of waste which reduces production costs in the short term, but harms the environment and will prove costly in the long term. They have often paid lip service to protecting trade secrets and other intellectual property rights and must be convinced that they will benefit from protecting intellectual property and making purchases from US entities to be a responsible player in the world economy and enable US consumers to remain as customers for their products.

China and the other Asian nations are developing an ever-increasing need for Middle East oil to fuel their economies. As the US becomes energy independent, China, which is a large Iranian oil customer will become a more important presence in Middle East politics and potential supporter of enemies of the US.

Although we must prepare for a potential confrontation with China, which has created serious doubts as to whether it can be trusted, we should be reaching out to work with China to promote the world economy and deal with the rogue countries and terrorist organizations that also pose a threat to China.

UNIONS

By the 1960s, labor unions, that had been so important in improving the working conditions and compensation of sweat-shop and assembly line workers were using their power to strike to gain benefits. Unions developed into large businesses that extracted large fees from their members, but often failed to act in a manner that was best for the employees they represented. Union demands for increased wages and benefits regularly resulted in employers negotiating an agreement to pay most of the excessive demands. The refusal of employers to meet extortionist union demands generally resulted in strikes that disrupted production. During the strike, union members were paid from a strike fund. However, they often failed to realize that the strike fund was their own money, collected from their pay and dissipated over the course of the strike.

Employers unable to carry on their operations and incurring daily losses did their best to hold out until the strike funds ran out but over time were pressured into giving in to union demands. Often, both union members and employers were losers based on final settlement terms. Employers then did their best to pass on the higher costs to consumers, leading to cost push inflation and stagflation.

Over time capital fled to areas where labor was cheaper and unions could be avoided. Our strongest industrial unions were in large part responsible for the bankruptcies of manufacturers in many of our most important industries (including the auto industry), leading to losses of millions of jobs held by union members. Regardless of outcomes in labor negotiations unions developed expensive overhead costs including high compensation packages for union executives paid for out of member's dues deducted from their wages.

Although they represent fewer workers, unions still have the power to disrupt some of our strongest businesses. For example, customers making major commitments when selecting a model for a fleet of airplanes place orders for delivery over a protracted number of years beginning years in the future. Many such customers consider placing orders with manufacturers located in other countries due to fear that untimely strikes by unions at

Boeing, which they have experienced in past years, will make it impossible for Boeing to make timely delivery of planes and spare parts. This was a major factor in Boeing's decision to build a multibillion-dollar non-union plant in South Carolina (while remaining in compliance with federal laws that are already excessively protective of the rights of union workers in the state of Washington). The opening of such new factory has been delayed by the outrageous politically motivated decision of the Obama appointees at the NLRB. President Obama and the NLRB seem oblivious to the fact that Airbus and other Boeing competitors are salivating and using the NLRB's action in their sales pitches to steer billions of dollars of future orders and tens of thousands of US jobs away from the US.

Many states have adopted right to work laws to seek to attract new non-union businesses. President Obama opposes such laws and has made it clear that he will propose rules to encourage union organization. Our public employee unions were later in arrival. Originally, most states banned strikes by public employees but over time this prohibition has generally been eliminated.

Public employee unions and their members view as earned through negotiation their excessive salaries and favorable contract terms including exceptionally high health care and retirement benefits granted by friendly or frightened politicians seeking votes or often extorted during or in anticipation of crippling strikes. With the passage of time, it is clear that because life expectancies are longer and retirement ages are too low, pension payments will be payable for more years than anticipated. Many public employee unions have extracted pensions benefits based on a percentage of the employee's final year of compensation, that is often greatly exaggerated by excessive overtime.

Public employees perform many important services for our society and should be fairly compensated but excessive salaries and pension and health care benefits threaten the solvency of many cities and states. Some municipalities have outsourced certain services to private companies to reduce cost by ridding their payrolls of unaffordable unionized workers.

Many fixed payment retirement benefits were negotiated in anticipation of tax revenue growth and investment income on funds set aside, which has not materialized. As a result many fixed benefit retirement plans offered by private companies have been converted to money purchase plans or 401(k)s. Unions have refused to modify their employee's plans. We must find a way to reduce the burden of excessive public employee health care and pension benefits. A return to prosperity and a higher rate of inflation will bring higher tax revenue and enable our states and cities to honor some contracts, but, we may have to face state and local bankruptcy reorganizations to reduce unrealistic public employee contract promises incapable of being kept. Cities have found that raising property taxes to meet rising obligations to public employees is difficult because many home mortgages are underwater or in foreclosure or because homeowners can move to another city with lower tax burdens, further reducing property values.

Now is the time to deal with future entitlements to avoid defaults on state and local securities and the third party risks associated with such defaults and the credit default swaps relating thereto. City and state governments should consider immediately replacing excessively compensated public employees who do not agree to reduce their benefits to fair and affordable compensation. The longer we wait, the worse the problem gets. President Obama and other Democrats received significant union support in recent elections and have opposed efforts by states to deal with excessive public employee compensation.

THE "TEA PARTY"

The so called "Tea Party" has been spawned because many well-intentioned Americans are concerned that the rapidly rising levels of entitlements and the national debt threaten the fiscal soundness of the US government. To its credit, the Tea Party movements sense the US faces a long-term debt problem resulting from entitlements and welfare payments, but they are generally clueless as to the actions we should take to stimulate the economy to generate revenues needed to control debt increases and to enable our government to service the debt. The Tea Party movements may have tried to emulate the Boston Tea Party, but their austerity proposals appear to come from parties at which British ladies enjoy tea and crumpets in the late afternoon, mostly talk about family values and economic concerns and not meaningful discussions about ways to promote economic growth.

The Tea Party is not a new cohesive party but a large number of disorganized and disparate groups largely comprised of conservative Republicans. They generally stress adopting austerity measures to reduce debt, but are clueless as to how macroeconomics works. Some of them seek to promote non-economic causes that may be popular among their constituencies but are not popular on a national level. Many of them believe that we should require a balanced budget. They are correct in wanting to control entitlement spending. However, they do not seem to understand that the only way to reduce a government's deficit is to grow the economy or that the goal should be to cause the economy to grow at a faster rate than the federal deficit grows. We must bring excessive entitlement spending and wasteful discretionary spending under control, but we must at the same time find ways to create jobs to grow the economy to increase tax revenues.

They look at the European financial crisis and worry that the US like Portugal, Italy, Ireland, Greece, and Spain (the "PIIGS countries"), will face financial insolvency if we do not curtail spending. They do not seem to understand that austerity measures like those propounded by some northern European leaders and being forced upon the PIIGS countries are causing the loss of more jobs and the government deficits in those southern European countries to be greater not smaller. The austerity policies are exacerbating a downturn in the European economies leading to a European recession and may still cause a worldwide downturn.

UNDERSTANDING MACROECONOMICS

Macroeconomics is counterintuitive. An individual with $1000 can save it in a bank, pay off debt, invest it or spend it. An individual consumer who spends less than all of his income increases his net worth. When the US Government reduces its spending it may not reduce its deficit. If it attempts to spend less it may discourage job creation and more people may lose their jobs. The result may be that the government receives less tax revenues and pays out more welfare benefits resulting in a larger deficit. Job creation-namely the creation of more than 20 million new or better jobs in the next ten years, and not austerity is vital to controlling the annual federal deficit and the national debt.

The federal government can safely afford to have significant debt, but at some level, which will be determined by the free market, there will be a flight from the dollar and spiraling interest rates leading to runaway inflation. The larger the national debt becomes the greater the danger that we will become subject to an interest rate upward spiral. The Federal government must try to prevent the rate of growth of the Federal deficit from increasing at a faster rate than the rate of growth of the GDP. The contrary has been true during the first 4 years of the Obama Administration, lost years for the US economy in large part because of the Great Recession but also because of President Obama's failed stimulus plan and the passage of Obamacare and Dodd-Frank.

The national debt grew by more than $6 trillion or more than 50% during the first four years of the Obama administration while the GDP grew only slightly after declining in 2009 during the Great Recession. In 2012 the national debt grew by about 7% while the GDP grew at an unacceptable rate of about 2%. As noted above the prospects for 2013 are not very promising, We need GDP growth of 5-10% per year for a period of years while restraining deficits to get our economy back on track.

Unfortunately, the stimulus plan of President Obama failed to generate the number of job increases needed to enable GDP growth to grow faster than the national debt. The poorly timed adoption of Obamacare has added an enormous unneeded entitlement and slowed business and job growth. It would help our GDP growth if most of Obamacare were repealed or substantially modified. To make matters worse, the Dodd-Frank legislation is causing banks to restrain lending and to lay-off employees.

ONE WORLD ECONOMY

We have one worldwide economy in the 21st century. There is no way to reverse the process nor should we want to do so. However, we can vastly improve the worldwide economy if we work together with Europe and the developing nations. China should not be looked at as our enemy. American capitalism and the American consumer have propelled the miracle of the Chinese and other emerging countries' economies. The Chinese and developing countries' prosperity has, in turn, prevented the collapse of the American and European economies into a devastating depression that would almost certainly have resulted from the horrendous banking practices which resulted in the Great Recession. In recent years China has from time to time shown signs of a slowdown resulting in part from the slowdown in demand in the US and Europe. If we work with Europe, China and the other emerging countries we can develop a world economy in the 21st century that can work together to control terrorism and improve the lives of substantially all the world's population.

ENERGY INDEPENDENCE

President Obama has from the inception of his presidency followed the advice of his environmental advisors and tried to convert US energy usage from fossil fuels to alternative green energy sources. He squandered billions of dollars on solar and other green energy projects while interfering with development of domestic sources of oil and gas. We have known throughout the term of the Obama presidency that we can make the US energy independent by promoting the use of natural gas. Despite a lack of support from the Obama administration and governmental interference, new fracking techniques have confirmed the existence of over a 100-year supply of natural gas reserves. The abundance in natural gas reserves and precipitous price decline is leading to a return of chemical and plastic manufacturing to the US. Fracking technology that time and again has been required to prove it satisfies water safety standards has also enabled the US to reverse its long-term decline in oil production.

During the election campaign President Obama took credit for the increase in natural gas and oil production, Such increase had occurred in large part on private lands under state-issued permits despite interference from the Obama administration that opposed almost all fossil fuel development. Fracking that generally takes place well below the earth's surface has both created jobs and provided a cheaper cleaner source of power than coal. It is a simple fact that many more jobs would have been created sooner by the oil and gas industry if President Obama's appointees had not impeded oil drilling and pipeline development and had supported the use of natural gas for transportation.

The growth in natural gas production has resulted in a sharp drop in the price of natural gas from over $13 to under $4 per MMBTU. The growth in oil production has not yet had as drastic a price effect because of market factors, but has lowered the domestic oil price substantially below the price of oil sold outside the US. Reduced natural gas and oil prices reduce business costs and act like a tax cut for consumers.

President Obama has the opportunity to enable the US to become energy independent during the current decade if his appointees approve drilling permits and pipelines to enable private entities to achieve that goal. Preventing BP from obtaining drilling permits after it has spent over $20 billion on cleaning up its past mistake will impede our becoming energy independent.

We should be offering tax credits to speed the construction of a national network of liquid natural gas supply stations for natural gas vehicles. Such stations are being developed along western highways even without governmental assistance because it is economically viable. Cities like NY and LA have recognized the tremendous advantages of using natural gas engines for buses and sanitation vehicles, that can be refueled at the city owned garages.

President Obama has again raised his concerns over global warming. We must remain diligent in promoting environmental controls to protect our environment. However, we must be prepared to delay certain environmental protections to enable us to avail ourselves of relatively safe energy sources to create jobs, promote prosperity, avoid the Great Recession from evolving into a depression and give us time and funding needed to create alternative energy sources.

GOVERNMENT REGULATION OF THE SECURITIES AND COMMODITIES MARKETS

Securities' Traders

In recent years the investment strategy of buying shares of strongly capitalized growth companies and holding them long term has lost favor to a trading mentality that attempts to take advantage of price swings resulting from worldwide economic news developments as well as earnings announcements and changes in projections. Stock market prices dominated by traders tend to be pushed upward to an excessive level often as the result of questionable corporate accounting practices followed by a sudden decline when some disappointing news appears.

Our securities markets are dominated by hedge funds, mutual funds and large traders who trade long and short positions, often with short-term horizons. Some traders have developed a risk-on, risk-off philosophy, which coupled with their high speed computer programs leads to large daily and sometimes sudden increases and declines in individual securities and ETFs. Traders take advantage of their computer programs to quickly respond to company news announcements and also anticipated effects of chart theory, short selling, margin calls and stop-loss orders.

In addition, private equity, which because of its success is attracting large investments from institutional clients and pension funds, is always looking for buying opportunities to take a company private to rehabilitate it and resell it to the public or another entity sometimes after creating new debt and draining out the available cash.

Short Selling and Stock Market Manipulation

Stock prices go up and down in cycles as investors make decisions to buy or sell based on many factors, including a variety of manipulative practices some of which are not illegal. Our regulators should attempt to limit the manipulative practices of traders, that have a serious effect on and greatly exaggerate price swings. However, our congressional leaders and the SEC seem incapable of understanding the egregious manipulative effects of short selling, when used in concert with chart theory, on securities trading. We tend to overlook the effects of short selling in a rising market when the line on the chart moves from the bottom left to the upper right – a chartist buy signal. However, short selling becomes a destructive force in a declining market or from time to time upon the price of an individual stock in a rising market.

Some investors use short selling to hedge risks by buying one stock in a market segment and selling short another stock in the same segment which they think is of a lesser relative value. This offers protection against general market declines or declines in the segment. They anticipate that even if both stocks decline, the shorted stock will decline by a greater percentage. This is one of a number of valid uses for short selling. However, the negatives caused by short selling on stock prices and economic damage that may be inflicted on the entities being shorted greatly outweigh the benefits of permitting unrestricted short selling.

Short selling can be and is often used as a manipulative device or practice. Short sellers have learned that when a company is in financial trouble, selling short at the same time as other short sellers offers the opportunity for large gains in the short run. Traders establish short positions, generally in stocks already subject to adverse disclosures, negative rumors and a declining stock price. They then rely on additional stock sales (including additional short sales by themselves or others) at ever declining prices to precipitate further stock market declines to a point where stop loss orders are executed, chart followers' sell points are reached, holders receive margin calls, tax loss selling comes into play and holders panic to drive stocks down.

After enhancing the decline in price of a security, the short sellers can sit back and wait for adverse business developments to affect the issuer as creditors and customers of the entity question its viability. Raising capital to meet a short-term need of the company whose stock has fallen precipitously may become impossible. The bankruptcy of the entity may result. We can only conjecture as to the extent of the damage caused by the bear raids of the short sellers on bank securities after the collapse of the mortgage and banking bubbles. Alternatively, even if the entity survives, the short sellers can step in and buy cheaply to cover their short positions.

The up-tick rule was designed during the Great Depression to prevent a repeat of bear raids by the "Robber Barons" who had large pools of money and used short sales at reducing prices to drive stocks down to induce margin calls (on stocks purchased under the then 10% margin requirement) so that they could come in and buy them at depressed prices. It is hard to believe that our securities regulators can be so ignorant as to fail to see the importance of the up-tick rule. The up-tick rule was flawed and needed strengthening because short sales placed a penny above the market could put a lid on the market price which prevented recovery, with the result that before long a downward sale would occur allowing the shorts to lower their offering price. The up-tick rule required some additional limits on short selling. It was an imperfect rule that should have been strengthened, not repealed.

The up-tick rule should be reinstated and adjusted to be more effective. For example, short selling should be prohibited in a rapidly declining stock or when the market price of a stock or relevant market averages have declined substantially from an identified level such as the 52 week high or the 50 or 200 day moving average. The role of short selling in computerized trading should be studied and better regulated. Though it may be difficult to enforce, the uptick rule should also be applied to trading in short derivative securities since they may contribute to a bear raid.

Why should you be able to sell a security you don't own? After all, except for certain restrictions relating to un-registered stock or stock held by insiders, 100% of all outstanding shares are always available for sale to prospective buyers. What benefit do we gain from encouraging manipulative action to cause stocks to go down even if they are temporarily overvalued? If an investor thinks a stock is overvalued he won't buy it or if he owns it he can sell it.

Short selling is so destructive to securities markets and has such a devastating effect on the capital needs and operations of entities caught in its manipulative web that we should probably ban short selling entirely.

The banking industry was devastated in 2007 and 2008 after the up-tick rule was eliminated and banks stock prices fell precipitously. It is impossible to measure the role played by traders, short sales and fraud and manipulation which resulted in the precipitous decline in value of bank securities, leading to the bankruptcy or disappearance of some of our largest banks and securities firms.

We will never know what would have happened if the up-tick rule had not been withdrawn by the SEC and short sellers had not celebrated daily while they ruthlessly drove down the price of shares of almost all of our banks and investment firms leading to the failure of Lehman Brothers and other large banks and brokerages and the takeover at depressed prices of Bear Stearns and Merrill Lynch.

Our incompetent regulatory agencies stood by helplessly as numerous over-leveraged investment firms and banks facing customer withdrawals and unable to sell assets or otherwise raise capital because of rapidly declining securities values became insolvent. Some speculators made fortunes from the bust and covered their shorts at pennies on the dollar. The Treasury Department stepped in to provide liquidity to the banking system only after it froze up following the collapse of Lehman Brothers.

Contrary to the argument put forth by the SEC (and short sellers), short selling does not level the playing field but creates a downward slope. It greatly expands the float, the number of shares of stock held by non-insiders not subject to a lock up and available to be offered for current sale. To understand how short selling increases the float, assume that Stockholder 1 owns 1000 shares of ABC common stock in street name held by Broker A. Another customer of Broker A decides to sell short 1000 shares of ABC stock, which are bought by Stockholder

2, and the 1000 Shares are delivered by Broker A to Broker B who is the broker of Stockholder 2. Stockholders 1 & 2 each own 1000 Shares of ABC stock, that is available for sale. Now the same short seller or another customer of Broker A or B or another brokerage sells an additional 1000 shares of ABC short. His broker must find the shares for delivery and calls Broker B, who lends the shares owned by Stockholder 2 to the short seller for delivery to Stockholder 3. Now three people believe they own the same 1000 shares.

It is true that the short sellers will at some future time have to cover and are potential buyers but they are not required to buy unless the stock goes up and they get a margin call or their broker needs the shares for delivery because they are called back by the lending broker. If bad news is announced or the market declines for any reason, then the same 1000 ABC shares may be offered for sale by Stockholders 1, 2 or 3. The short sellers who are benefitting from the decline may have excessive margin credit to allow them to sell more shares short into a falling market. They may sense the opportunity to set off a series of stop loss orders, sell orders from chart theory followers or margin calls against the long positions of Stockholder 1, 2 or 3 or other stockholders.

Brokers charge large fees for lending the shares to the short sellers, that they are not required to share with customers who own the shares if the shares are held in a margin account. They do not seem to care if the shares of ABC that are loaned out to the short sellers are sold driving down the price of the shares. No broker should be able to lend a customer's shares to a short seller without offering its customer shareholder a fee for lending the shares and the right to prevent the loan of his shares.

The broker is facilitating a sale that is detrimental to its customer who owns the stock. The short seller is by his very sale putting downward pressure on the stock the customer wants to go up. When your stock is loaned, the buyer of the short security gets ownership of and the right to vote your security. Although the short seller must compensate you for any dividends you are entitled to receive on the borrowed stock, such compensation is not a qualified dividend and is taxable at ordinary income rates. On occasion your broker will offer you compensation for lending your shares, but the detriment may often outweigh the benefit.

The SEC should continually investigate whether traders are complying with the requirement that they arrange for stock to be available for delivery before making naked short sales. The fact that you cover the short a few seconds later doesn't cure the violation. There is a question whether the flash crash may have involved short sales where the stock to be delivered was not previously identified.

Although short sellers generally drive a stock price down, on some occasions short sellers get trapped and drive an overpriced stock even higher. On occasion a stock with a very large short position in a rising market goes up in price and becomes subject to a "short squeeze" resulting from short sellers who are unable to meet margin calls being forced to buy in the stock, driving it higher.

Some European governments have enacted rules to limit short selling of bank securities, but the SEC ignores the ability of short sellers to drive stocks down and cause periods of panic among investors. Although the prices of bank securities have enjoyed a small rebound, the increased prices will make them more vulnerable during the next downturn. Short sellers of bank securities who remember the rapid decline of bank stocks during 2007 and 2008 and are aware of the sell signals of chart theorists and the expected existence of stop loss orders a few points below market prices and other market factors could precipitate a new bank crisis at any time. The claims by our large banks that they are now soundly financed are based on questionable estimates of the value of mortgages, MBSes and other derivatives. Not enough has been changed to prevent history from repeating itself.

Chart Theory

Educated by TV programs, a growing number of investors study charts to help them make buy/sell decisions. Chart theory, that graphically presents and analyzes stock price and trading volume movements over time periods, takes many forms. Chart theorists believe they can use charts showing past sale prices to detect the buy/sell decisions of large investors or groups of investors whose acquisitions or sales of a security are affecting and may continue to affect a stock's price movement. They rely on breakouts up or down from certain selected trigger price points on the chart as signals they should buy or sell a security.

One problem with chart theory is that it often becomes a self-fulfilling prophecy. Tens of thousands of investors studying the same charts decide to buy or sell a security at the same time, inducing rapid and large price swings. Few traders get the price they want as the market is instantly overwhelmed by orders from chartists. Some traders use stop loss orders above or below sell points on the charts to protect against losses. When such stop loss orders are executed they often drive a stock down triggering a chart sell signal. Short sellers often study charts to look for sell signals and either short just before the sell point on the chart or pile on shorts after the sell signal is indicated by the chart. With the elimination of the up-tick rule, it is much easier for short sellers acting like cattle rustlers to start a stampede to cash in on declining stock prices resulting from chart theory sell signals, stop loss orders, margin calls and panic. It is highly likely that short selling (combined with chart theory) was a leading cause of the sustained drop in the price of Apple shares at the end of 2012.

Chart theory is arguably protected by freedom of speech. However, it sometimes has the same effect on the price of a stock as shouting "fire" in a movie theater. The SEC seems to be oblivious to its effects on the markets. It should be diligent to study the release of false information about a company that is designed to cause a buy or sell chart signal to be acted upon. It should also carefully monitor market action following a chart theory buy or sell signal to identify whether other manipulative practices are being used contemporaneously.

Chart theorists rarely tell investors how difficult it is to interpret a chart or how often a buy or sell signal works to the disadvantage of a chart follower because of unanticipated events.

Circuit Breakers

The SEC has adopted and from time to time modified circuit breakers to try to prevent excessive short term swings in securities' prices, avoid panic and allow sound heads to prevail. The required price drop before the circuit breakers come into play and the length of the down time is geared to limit trading restraints and allow the prompt resumption of the trading markets to promote liquidity. The current circuit breaker rules adopted by the SEC to suspend securities trading for short periods during precipitous price declines are likely to prove of little or no value. They might even accelerate panic selling. Circuit breakers would have a much better chance of success if linked with automatic bans on short selling for periods before or after the circuit breakers go into effect.

Stop Loss Orders

Stop loss orders are of questionable value. They are not dependable enough to rely on. If the stop loss order becomes a market order when the stop loss price is reached, the market price may be falling rapidly (because of adverse news, short selling or chart theorist selling) and you may get a lesser price than expected from the sale. Your stop loss price can be hit during a downward break in a volatile market and the price of the stock may recover even before you know your shares have been sold. If you require a sale at the stop loss price your order may not be executed.

The combination of stop loss orders and sales by chartists and short sellers once precipitated may create an effect similar to falling dominos leading to a rapidly declining stock price.

DELAWARE CORPORATE LAW

Delaware law, as interpreted by Delaware courts grants almost unlimited discretion to the board of directors. The principle responsibility of the board of directors of a corporation is to the stockholders. Corporations have compensation committees to determine the salaries of their executives. Many of our corporations are operated like private clubs that are controlled by boards of directors that vastly overpay the executive officers. They also permit them to take excessive risks (which members of the board of directors often do not understand). Boards of directors of Delaware corporations reward executives who lay off employees to enhance profits while at the same time they approve excessive compensation packages for executives reducing profits. The change in the US income tax laws punishing cash compensation in excess of $1,000,000 actually encouraged excessive non-cash compensation to executives.

Outrageous contracts with excessive compensation or termination pay have been upheld by Delaware courts as being within the discretion of the board of directors, who often retain the services of accountants and lawyers to write expensive opinions purchased to help them justify payment of excessive compensation. It is easy to justify a small (or in some cases a large) percentage increase to a CEO when you compare it to the most excessive compensation you can find which is being paid to a competitor's CEO. Boards rarely attempt to claw back bonuses or stock profits gained from fraudulent SEC filings even if they leave the corporation subject to class action lawsuits.

Hedge funds and mutual funds are taking a larger say in selection of the board members of companies they invest in, but they have a trader's mentality, which favors showing short term profit increases (whether or not based on questionable estimates and failure to set up proper reserves). They often approve excessive executive compensation in stock or stock options under a plan designed to have management focus on short-term earnings increases.

Our corporations are created under state law but they are subject to the federal securities' laws. It is often difficult to measure the importance a CEOs' decisions in the success of a corporation. We sometimes question whether the directors are honoring their responsibility when we look at the excessive compensation packages including stock option grants, bonuses, pension benefits and termination pay paid to executives.

Corporate executives of non-union entities often feel no responsibility to non-executive employees. Faced with rising health care costs (which when paid by the employer represent a form of increased employee compensation), corporations are hesitant to give cash raises to employees. They even reduce payrolls as necessary to be able to show an increase in short-term profits.

Although some corporations offer higher compensation packages to attract and motivate better qualified employees, at a time of high unemployment levels employees often have limited mobility or bargaining power. We should try to find a way to encourage or require corporations to more fairly allocate compensation between executives and non-management employees. Encouraging employees to unionize is not the solution. Unions have severely damaged American manufacturers to the detriment of both the stockholders and union members.

Corporations have been increasing profitability by controlling payroll costs except for excessive compensation paid to executives. Although large salaries, bonuses and stock grants given to a few executives may in the aggregate represent a small percentage of total compensation, disproportionately high compensation to executives is unfair to stockholders and other employees. Compensation committees should have to consider the compensation of all employees when determining the compensation of executives. Although it would be difficult to establish the appropriate standards, compensation committees should have to justify in a writing to be filed as an exhibit to the company's annual report their allocation of compensation and benefits between non-executive and executive employees particularly if they are only increasing the compensation or benefits of executive employees. Wage increases paid out of a portion of increasing profits to non-executive employees would benefit the middle class and promote consumer spending and increases in the GDP. We might encourage corporations to better treat their non-executive employees by offering a federal income tax credit to entities offering compensation increases to such employees.

THE MIDDLE CLASS AND THE HOUSING CRISIS

The US Constitution created an environment in which every person in the US has an opportunity to work hard to provide a good life for his or her family and in some cases become wealthy. Beginning after World War II, it has enabled a class of individuals to be able to afford to acquire assets, including a home, a car and discretionary items, and to lead a reasonably comfortable life. Such persons are loosely defined as the middle class. The amount needed to achieve middle class status varies in different cities across the US, as the cost of housing, food and other items is much higher in our most successful urban areas. For many years after the end of World War II we witnessed a strong growth of the middle class, which ended with the loss of numerous manufacturing jobs to the developing nations and from labor saving technological developments. The bursting of the banking and housing bubbles has had a devastating effect on the middle class.

For more than 50 years, until 2007, the family home often over time became the family's most valuable asset. The goal of most young American men (the "American Dream") was to get a good paying job, get married, work hard and save enough to acquire a home and enjoy and improve it while raising a family. Each month you made a payment that slowly reduced the principal amount of your mortgage, that generally had a 30-year term. As an increasing number of women joined the workforce they supplemented family income. More often than not, the increasing equity in your home when added to the portion of the income from your job(s) you were able to save and invest enabled you and your family to become members of the "middle class."

The "middle class" was a difficult-to-define group of individuals who were able to accumulate wealth over time and who generally lived a more comfortable life than their parents. During the last half of the 20th century, the number of middle class families grew, working members got raises, made home improvements, bought cars and TVs. Single-parent families and unmarried individuals joined the middle class. The US economy grew and an increasing number of members of the middle class were even able to buy, improve and enjoy second homes, boats and other recreational vehicles and equipment, adding to their wealth and quality of life.

You often improved your home with improvements installed by your own labor and proudly raised your family in it. With normal inflation of 2 to 4 percent (and sometimes higher) per year and repayment of mortgage principal over 15 to 30 years, you established an important source of wealth, leaving you with various options. One option was to sell the home upon retirement and use the proceeds to move to a less expensive retirement community and help finance your retirement.

Few people understood that a portion of the middle class wealth was unrealistic because it came from excessive wages and benefits extorted by unions from our manufacturers, who over a period of years because of cost pressures and mismanagement were unable to compete in the highly competitive late 20th century worldwide economy.

As a result of declining income and the collapse of the housing bubble, the American Dream of home ownership is having a disastrous ending for too many families. Greedy and incompetent bankers and left-leaning politicians have turned housing from a dream to a nightmare for an unacceptably large portion of our population. Along the way they have severely damaged the banking system and brought the home construction industry to a standstill. The inability of housing prices to make more than a partial recovery in most markets has left the banking system saddled with defaulted and under-reserved mortgages, MBSes of questionable value and related litigation claims.

At the beginning of this century the housing and mortgage bubbles had temporarily created large numbers of construction jobs and masked manufacturing job losses and the stagnant pay of manufacturing employees. The collapse of housing prices and the Great Recession that inevitably followed is a national catastrophe. From the exaggerated bubble prices, housing losses alone total many trillions of dollars that has driven many members out of the middle class into poverty. The current overhang of over five million abandoned and foreclosed homes and homes in foreclosure or facing potential foreclosure or with upside down mortgages is preventing a strong rebound in home construction needed to spur job creation and a recovery from the Great Recession. The financial problems of our municipalities have been exacerbated by the excess compensation commitments our municipalities have made to their employees, which have led to increases in property tax rates (on often declining assessed valuations) and declining services. It is no wonder that young families are hesitant to buy their first home even if they can afford it.

Members of the middle class who relied on home ownership have seen their wealth devastated by a reduction in both income and wealth as the value of homes and retirement funds have declined.

Some members of the middle class do not rely on home ownership to maintain or grow their wealth, but it is almost impossible for most middle class Americans to replace the home as an investment vehicle. The overhang of foreclosures continues to haunt the housing and banking industries. Until we find a way to stimulate a recovery in the housing market without large numbers of additional foreclosures, we will continue to deprive a substantial portion of our population from becoming or remaining members of the middle class.

The government played an important role in the banking and housing collapse. Incompetent government agencies failed to regulate the banks or the securities markets. Left-leaning Democrats and political activists encouraged the making of improvident high-risk loans to support their political ambitions and/or in some cases well-intentioned social views. They didn't realize that encouraging and in some cases strong-arming banks into giving credit to unqualified borrowers who later found themselves in default, would cause great pain and distress for the borrowers and their families, and was creating a systemic risk of collapse for the banking and housing industries. Too many homes were built and purchased by families who couldn't afford them.

Home buyers and the investors who purchased the mortgages and MBSes bought into the ridiculous argument (propounded by bank executives making tens of millions of dollars a year who were supposed to be acting in the best interest of the stockholders and creditors of the bank) that with normal inflation housing could only continue to go up in value. Bankers argued that regardless of the mortgagor's credit standing, mortgages could be refinanced or foreclosed to enable the lenders and owners of MBSes to profit. Mortgages and MBSes that should have been rated as junk were, for a fee paid to rating agencies, given undeserved AAA ratings.

The SEC ignored the banks' and mortgage companies' irresponsible lending practices and the grossly excessive profits reported by banks as a result of their failure to provide for adequate loss reserves. The banks and mortgage companies justified increased use of leverage based on fraudulently claimed profitability. Excess leverage greatly amplified the losses when the true value of the improvidently granted mortgages was exposed. The government has compounded the problem by failing to prosecute the bank and mortgage company executives who made millions of dollars from their fraudulent and grossly negligent conduct. We did not need new laws to regulate the banks, we needed to enforce the existing laws. The Dodd-Frank legislation has given bankers legitimate arguments against unfair and excessive government regulation and created a debate that has given cover to the wrongdoers who violated the laws that existed before Dodd-Frank.

There is a separate and distinct story relating to each mortgage that has been foreclosed, is in default or is under water. Some had small or no down payments and very little skin in the game and little to lose by buying the home they could afford to carry only at artificially low interest rates. Many speculators who could buy a home with little or no investment risk and who made large profits flipping homes as home prices climbed during the bubble period, failed to close and lost their deposit or defaulted on non-recourse mortgages and abandoned homes as prices declined. Other buyers could afford a down payment but took advantage of teaser interest rates on loans they knew they couldn't pay after interest rates reset. They counted on home price inflation and refinancing.

At the extreme, some purchasers put nothing down (or might have received a rebate exceeding the down payment), made no improvements in the home, signed subprime mortgages often requiring no principal and low interest payments, defaulted in making their mortgage payment when their mortgage reset and couldn't be refinanced, and stopped paying association dues and local property taxes and water charges and are now living rent free, fighting eviction and looking for a government bailout. They have money to spend for other purposes. Others had ample means, made a 20% down payment and are paying their mortgage. The remaining individual stories lie somewhere in between, with many homeowners suffering because of the decline in home prices, vacancies in their neighborhoods or the deterioration of their neighbors' homes. Some regardless of their down payment, moved in and spent substantial amounts to improve the home expecting to be able to enjoy it for many years but are now unable or unwilling to pay an upside down mortgage. Mortgage loans were often made based on fraudulent appraisals and fraudulent or no document loan applications, many of which were monitored by untrained or dishonest mortgage brokers who were paid substantial fees to supply the mortgage flow needed by the MBS sellers.

Our government has let the banks and homeowners suffer with the problems. Too many families who reasonably expected to be able to afford their home are under unrelenting financial stress. They have seen their entire savings wiped out as their incomes have evaporated, stagnated or declined and home prices have eroded.

Some borrowers were promised by bankers, mortgage brokers, real estate brokers or builders that they would be able to refinance and didn't understand the risk of years later being told by bankers that they are unable to refinance because they do not qualify under current market conditions. Our bankers ignored the risk of making bad loans because they were able to sell them to FNMA or Freddie Mac or securitize them and sell them to unsuspecting investors. Many also thought they would be protected by housing inflation, late fees, resetting interest rates and prepayment penalties. They ignored the possibility of the bubble breaking, leading to a material decline in home prices. They also ignored the litigation that would inevitably follow when mortgage and MBS investors demanded rescission or compensation for their losses.

During the housing bubble as the price of homes soared, many homeowners used their homes as an ATM machine and refinanced to the maximum amount possible. Banks were eager to refinance at ever increasing loan amounts to earn prepayment penalties and other fees or as payment problems arose to merely avoid default. Some borrowers used the proceeds to buy sports cars, pay for vacations or for ordinary living expenses or to pay off credit card balances. They then had borrowing power, which they quickly used. Such spendthrift homeowners often lived next door to families living the American Dream who saved for years before making a substantial down payment on a home and then made timely mortgage payments. Many of them later found that their equity had been wiped out as home prices fell in their often blighted neighborhood. Few people understood or anticipated the financial risk of home ownership that might result if and when the housing bubble burst and housing prices collapsed.

It is no surprise that many homeowners have given up trying to maintain their home ownership and are failing to make payments on their mortgages, pay their real estate taxes, water and sewer bills or coop or condo association assessments. Instead of making capital investments to enable them to enjoy and increase the long-term value of their homes, they are permitting the homes to deteriorate and making only those repairs as are absolutely necessary. Some of them are (i) recouping part of their losses by remaining in the homes until they are legally evicted without making any payments or (ii) raising cash by stripping their homes, selling appliances and plumbing fixtures, further reducing the home's value. They are destroying neighborhoods. Others are abandoning their homes that in some neighborhoods are subject to looting. At the same time, many homeowners with underwater mortgages they are unable to refinance are standing by their legal commitment and paying their mortgages on time despite unfair interest rates. They deserve assistance.

Some homeowners live in fear of personal liability resulting from a foreclosure proceeding and are seeking to settle their obligations, often for significantly reduced amounts, by means of short sales. Other homeowners do not seem to care about their already damaged credit ratings or moral issues relating to deliberately defaulting. Consumer spending and the GDP are getting a short-term benefit from the extra funds available to the homeowners who temporarily are able to get away without paying for housing.

Our bankers dealing with foreclosures have once again demonstrated their sloppiness, incompetence and willingness to let their employees commit fraud. Many banks, that never completed or couldn't locate required documentation, used automated signatures ("robo-signing") of officers to certify facts that entitled them to commence foreclosure actions. When the practice was disclosed and used as a defense by homeowners to delay foreclosure, the bank foreclosure attempts were often thrown out of court. A large number of foreclosure actions delayed for years are now beginning to be brought or moved forward by banks. Homes sold at foreclosure generally bring substantially lower sales prices than comparable homes being sold in the neighborhood putting further downward pressure on home prices. Banks could limit their losses by making a deal with and taking title in a short sale from the homeowner prior to the foreclosure sale or could buy the home in the foreclosure proceeding and hold it for resale at a higher price or for rental. In many cases, the bank would have to create or expand a staff and fund this operation. They seem incapable of dealing in a prudent business manner with the problem and prefer to just take excessive losses with each foreclosure.

Entities are now being formed and well capitalized by investors to purchase foreclosed homes for rental and resale. If we stand aside they will gobble up the foreclosed homes at prices generally well below market prices in the area and profit at the expense of the homeowner and banks.

Brokers have recently taken to the airwaves to attempt to convince potential buyers that home prices are now rising and they will miss the boat if they do not buy now. They may be right but they are distracting our regulators from the fact that we still have millions of underwater and defaulted mortgages awaiting foreclosure. Housing prices will eventually stabilize, but housing prices must rise significantly to have an effect on homeowners with upside down mortgages.

What is happening in the market place may be a way in which capitalism cleanses the system and allows housing to bottom, but it is not good for our country and there has to be a better way to end the housing collapse.

The collapse in housing prices is unprecedented in US history. It has decimated the wealth and retirement plans of Americans, including many who have no mortgage on their home. The housing collapse and the sudden decline in the value of the mortgages that financed the housing bubble has led to the insolvency of many of the world's largest banks and was the principle cause of the Great Recession, which resulted in significantly reduced federal and state tax revenues. It has accelerated and compounded the looming problem of paying for our important entitlements and has increased the urgency for dealing with the long term financial problems of our federal and state and local governments.

The housing collapse is a cancer we should have attacked years ago rather than trying half-hearted attempts to refinance a limited number of mortgages for owners with equity in their homes and who were current in making their mortgage payments. Many potential buyers who would like to become homeowners postpone a home purchase because they fear their down payment will disappear or can't qualify for a mortgage. Others postpone making a long-term financial commitment because they fear the potential loss of their job.

Banks that engaged in or carelessly permitted fraudulent loan practices and whose inept mortgage procedures and record keeping, complex and in some cases unenforceable collateralized mortgage securitization agreements, failure to properly record mortgage transfers and fraudulent foreclosure practices (including the use of robo signing) are being prevented from capping their losses by foreclosing and selling the properties. On the other hand, some banks postponed foreclosures to hide their losses (particularly on home equity loans) hoping that prices would recover or they could establish loss reserves over time.

Although they are now better but not adequately capitalized for the risks they are taking, the banks remain subject to attack from a never-ending number of public officials with political ambitions and lawyers representing private claimants seeking recoveries based on the past frauds that caused trillions of dollars of losses. Outrageous scandals such as the Libor rate manipulation keep coming out of the woodwork. They do not seem capable of clearing the slate no matter how many billions they pay in settlements.

The recent politically motivated action brought by the NYS Attorney General against JP Morgan Chase, whose stockholders have already suffered large mortgage related losses, is a shotgun attack (which the NYS Attorney General believes will be easier to win than an action against the responsible individuals) for actions prior to its acquisition of Bear Stearns, which the US government induced it to acquire.

We will be unable to end the housing crisis without the return of housing inflation. Actions by the Fed after the collapse of the banking and housing bubbles clearly indicate that the Fed was concerned that deflation was damaging housing and the banking system. The Fed's QE1, QE2 and QE3 programs were directed to strengthening the banks and preventing a deflationary spiral. We note that the Fed's zero interest rate policies have promoted oil, food and commodities inflation but until recently have had little noticeable effect on housing inflation except to stop the decline in home prices.

Modest housing inflation has returned in some markets because individual buyers and entities organized by private equity that seek to rent the homes for a profit are purchasing them for cash (avoiding mortgage hang-ups) and because a limited number of potential buyers believe they are missing out on the available bargains.

New home construction has shown some minor improvement. The construction cost of building a new home has been reduced despite the increased cost of acquiring construction materials because the value of vacant land has declined precipitously. Housing demand in selected cities is benefitting from purchases for investment (sometimes at very high prices) by foreign investors from China, Russia and South and Central American countries. New homes will be built to replace the thousands of homes destroyed by hurricane Sandy.

President Obama and his advisors almost certainly failed to recognize at the time of his election that the housing crisis was different than any in our country's history. Never before were so many homeowners overextended and unable to pay their mortgages without the refinancing relief they had counted on. Add to that the number homeowners who lost their job and their income and could no longer afford home ownership, but couldn't sell because they had no equity. The lack of equity is preventing some homeowners from relocating.

A couple of years ago the Obama administration came up with the first of a number of almost worthless proposals to get mortgage holders to give mortgage relief to an insignificant number of mortgagors. We ask ourselves why President Obama has watched homeowners with underwater mortgages suffer for so long without a serious attempt to help them. Probably because he isn't being blamed for the mess and it is too difficult for his advisers to understand and deal with the complex problems. Possibly it is because he seems to only care about the poor who own few homes and despite his repeated claims to the contrary, doesn't align himself with the middle class. After attending college and law school on scholarships, he went in a short period of time from being poor to being rich and effectively skipped being middle class.

When President Obama took office, many felt that only a limited percentage of mortgages would default. He probably wasn't advised that as mortgages go underwater, homeowners fail to maintain their homes and some, even if they have available funds, don't pay their mortgages or real estate taxes. As houses become blighted and sold at very depressed prices on foreclosure, the disease spreads to neighboring homes, which also decline in value.

Now years later the Fed is attempting to strengthen the banks and promote bank lending by providing virtually interest-free loans to the insolvent banks. But why should banks lend? Lending to homeowners and small businesses has proven to be loss generating. They can borrow from the Fed and buy higher interest rate medium term US government bonds, which have only a limited interest rate risk.

QE1, QE2 and QE3 were used to keep interest rates low to help generate a housing and stock market recovery and to give a present to the banks to strengthen their capital accounts. Our Government should have required the banks to share their present from the Fed with homeowners in the form of significant mortgage relief. Such a requirement would have raised the constitutional issue as to whether mortgage holders could be required to give up their contractual rights and adjust their mortgages at the request of the mortgagor.

Since relief from debt is permitted under the federal bankruptcy laws, there should be no problem modifying federal bankruptcy laws or creating a new federal mortgage law to establish new mortgage courts with power to deal with granting mortgage relief by reducing the principal amount and changing the terms and conditions of existing mortgages. It would represent a drastic change in the states' long recognized mortgage laws. It is needed because the multi-trillion problem orchestrated by the lenders has been permitted to fester and has damaged local real estate markets, the US economy and the lives of millions of American families.

Despite claims by bank executives as to the financial strength of our banking system, we will not have a sound banking system until we stabilize the housing market because many banks still have a high percentage of their assets invested in underwater home mortgages.

To restore the housing dream so vital to the lifestyle and financial health of generations of Americans we must find a way to deal with (i) the millions of homes that are subject to unfair, defaulted or upside down mortgages, (ii) issues relating to title and control of the mortgages in question because of shoddy banking practices, and (iii) situations where the amount of the monthly mortgage debt payments (interest plus amortization) exceed the homeowners ability to pay because the homeowners signed mortgages they knew or should have known they were unable to pay from the start and were hoping they would be able to refinance.

Although they have increased their loss reserves, some banks are unwilling or unable to grant mortgage relief for reasons including the following:

(i)   They believe they can limit their losses by dragging their feet and continue to collect excessive interest from homeowners who are paying their mortgages,

(ii) They can't resolve complex mortgage ownership issues which they negligently or fraudulently created,

(iii) They would be required to recognize a loss based on the value they are carrying the mortgage on their books, or

(iv) They believe (with good cause) that even if they reduce the interest rate or forgive or postpone a part of the principal, many of the mortgages will go back into default.

Subordinate mortgage holders are impeding foreclosures because they don't want to acknowledge that many of their loans are worthless and realize their losses.

A Plan To Cure The Housing Cancer

The collapse of the housing and mortgage bubbles has severely damaged the American economy and may yet lead us into a depression. Our politicians and government officials helped the banks survive but they have no answers to the housing problem. Except for a few insignificant efforts to stimulate a housing recovery, they sat on their hands watching as housing prices declined. Many homeowners, banks and mortgage companies have been destroyed financially. Housing prices in many areas declined by 30-35%, that appears to be a bottom. A recovery in housing prices is taking place in some parts of the country. Select areas like Miami and New York are witnessing a boom as a result of foreign buyers who are in some cases buying very expensive homes. Many people think we are witnessing a normal boom and bust cycle, disregarding the outrageous behavior that caused the current aberration in housing prices. Owning a home in the US before the turn of the current century was generally a sound, low risk investment. It is no longer true today for too many homeowners.

We cannot wait an additional five to ten years or more for the housing market to rebound significantly. Homeowners making payments on underwater mortgages are losing hope that they will ever be able to recover a significant portion of their investment. Each time a mortgage is foreclosed, a family loses its home and the homeowner must recognize the loss of his entire investment. The family is forced to find alternative housing and family life, including the children's education, is disrupted.

Purchases by investors are beginning to dent the glut of homes for sale. Some individuals sense an opportunity to buy homes at distressed prices in foreclosure and renovate and rent the homes for profit. Opportunistic hedge funds and private equity are also buying foreclosed homes for resale and rental. Housing prices in most markets have stopped falling and might even recover 20% or more, but that will leave millions of homes either foreclosed or underwater with upside down mortgages. It should not be considered an acceptable solution for wealthy investors to buy homes that are being foreclosed at extremely depressed prices to profit from bank's taking excessive losses and homeowners losing their entire life's savings.

The changes proposed below are complex. Many banks and individuals will object to the proposed changes on the basis of contract law. Many will not appreciate the urgency of curing the housing cancer to the survival of the middle class.

Congress already has a full plate of issues such as the debt ceiling, sequestration, unemployment, a stagnant economy, and major debt and entitlement issues including Obamacare. It is going to be faced with a choice with regard to housing which is important for job creation. It can and in all likelihood will take no action relating to housing and let home owners continue to suffer and lose their investment while new investors make bargain purchases. Alternatively it can take bold steps to correct the housing crisis and avoid the risk that weak housing construction will delay or prevent an economic recovery. The current demand for expensive housing from foreign investors who buy for cash may be a temporary phenomenon. It is helping builders, but is not solving the mortgage crisis

If we fail to do so or to find an alternative solution to the housing problem when the next downturn in the US economy appears, it may unless Congress promptly approves large stimulus spending (which is unlikely because of the growing national debt) lead us into a deep recession or even a depression with 20% or higher unemployment.

We must consider modification of our mortgage laws to prevent the lenders who were the principal cause of the housing bubble and crash that followed from dragging their feet to prevent refinancing of underwater mortgages. We must consider giving all homeowners the opportunity to demand refinancing on fair terms. By enabling them to do so we will be providing assistance to the middle class and create conditions which will greatly reduce the number of foreclosures and lead to a sound housing recovery.

Our banks will actually benefit by having the mortgages reduced but guaranteed by a US government agency because it will reduce lender losses to amounts below which they should have already reserved against.

One reason that our president and Congress have done very little to deal with the housing crisis is that the issues are extremely complex. The wrongdoing by bankers, congressmen, broker/dealers, mortgage brokers, real estate agents, builders and mortgage applicants was so extensive and took so many forms that it is extremely difficult and in some cases impossible to determine whether the homeowner was at fault in connection with the issuance of the now defaulted or underwater mortgages. Arguments have been made for offering or excluding assistance to homeowners. Inaction is prolonging and worsening the crisis and impeding the recovery from the Great Recession.

Rather than spending additional years in an attempt to deal with blame and the ethical and moral hazard issues and trying to determine which of our current homeowners deserve government assistance in modifying their mortgages and which do not, we must find a way to revive the housing market irrespective of who was at fault. We must come up with a solution that can be offered to all current homeowners who, regardless of past conduct, can afford to and are willing to pay a fair rental equivalent based on the current fair market value of their home. The sole exceptions should be very large mortgages or mortgages given to collateralize a business indebtedness and the limited number of cases where it can be proven that a homeowner was guilty of criminal fraud (requiring a finding of guilt beyond a reasonable doubt as distinguished from civil fraud, which can be based on a preponderance of the evidence) in the mortgage application.

Some Americans are greatly concerned with the size of the national debt. Because of the Great Recession and rapid growth of the national debt we must find a housing solution that, like TARP loans, is revenue positive for the government over the long run. That goal should be achievable because homes have throughout history proven to be assets of lasting value that despite normal wear and tear can be maintained and even improved at reasonable expense by the homeowner. Because of inflation, homes have prior to the Great Recession generally increased in value over time. The current inventory of unsold homes resulting from the excess number of homes built during the housing bubble and the Great Recession will be absorbed over time from current needs, population growth and family formations.

We can reasonably anticipate that over the next 10 to 20 years with even moderate housing inflation home prices if unburdened from high rates of foreclosures will recover and may even reach new highs.

There is a way to cure the housing cancer without giving houses away to investors at bargain prices or waiting 10-20 years and praying for an economic recovery, which is being impeded by the housing crisis. It will require Congress to legislate a drastic change in our mortgage laws with a focus on helping homeowners who will be empowered to initiate the process of restructuring their mortgages. It will create a win, win, win solution for all directly involved homeowners, lienholders and the US taxpayers.

We should devise a plan to offer assistance to distressed homeowners. It should include a qualification procedure they can easily understand and comply with and that will enable them to enjoy living in their home at a fair cost and to recover their investment in their home and earn a profit over time.

To accomplish this, we must pass federal laws (based on bankruptcy law principles) that require banks and other mortgage holders to modify existing mortgages. This will give a substantial number of homeowners with underwater or defaulted mortgages an opportunity to retain their homes. This can be done in a manner that enables the mortgage holders the opportunity in most cases to limit their losses on their existing loan portfolio while resolving the housing crisis and encouraging sound lending practices in the future. We must assure taxpayers that the US government agency to be created for the purpose will make a profit over time on its investment if the prices of homes recover even modestly.

The proposed law should reduce the monthly cost to the homeowner so that the homeowner pays an amount that will

- Pay all mortgages on his home having an aggregate principal amount equal to the fair market value ("FMV") of the home at a market interest rate in constant monthly payments over a 30-year term.

- Cover the cost of related homeowner payments (the "Related Homeowner Payments" or "RHPs"), including local taxes and assessments, condo, coop or association charges, casualty insurance premiums, and water and sewer charges, as applicable.

Achieving this objective will require drastic changes in federal law relating to home mortgages. Exceptional leadership from President Obama or some members of Congress is going to be vital to get the mortgage relief proposed herein understood, debated and enacted into law. Congress must demonstrate that it is capable of dealing with multiple problems at the same time.

We must expedite a concerted nonpartisan effort to pass a new Federal mortgage law ("FML") based upon the following considerations:

1. We should create a mortgage relief program ("MRP") under which a participating homeowner may now or in the future reduce the aggregate principal amount of the mortgages on his home to the FMV of the home and obtain a modification of the terms of any outstanding mortgage. Every homeowner who has owned a home with a mortgage that has been in force for at least two year will be eligible to voluntarily participate in the program unless (i) the aggregate mortgages and liens on the home exceed $3 Million, (ii) the mortgage was given to collateralize a business loan, or (iii) the homeowner has been found guilty of criminal fraud in connection with their obtaining the mortgage. We must end the debate over who deserves assistance. Almost all homeowners should be able to seek equitable relief. We must end the crisis even if it means we have to offer to help people who were not qualified for home ownership, who squandered the equity in their home by refinancing their mortgage or through home equity loans or who had some degree of fault for their mortgage application containing false information or

whose mortgages or other home related payments are in default. They were encouraged to do so by bankers and brokers. We should proceed with attempts to punish the wrongdoers, but we cannot delay resolving the housing crisis. The availability of an MRP will encourage banks to engage in sound lending practices in the future, which will likely lead to a return to a substantial down payment requirement. It will discourage banks from extending high-risk home equity loans and from unreasonably refinancing and adding to the principal amount of the mortgage as home prices rise.

2. To facilitate the granting of relief to homeowners and overcome existing title problems, a new federal court (or branch of the United States Bankruptcy Court), known as the US Mortgage Court ("USMC"), should be established by Congress. The USMC shall have joint jurisdiction with state courts over title issues (which shall remain subject to state laws) and all mortgages and liens against the homes of participating homeowners (which shall remain subject to existing state or federal laws except to the extent that the new FML specifically overrides existing laws.)

3. All homeowners who elect to participate and seek relief under the MRP shall be required to deliver preliminary proof of home ownership, (which may simply be a copy of a mortgage statement), and agree to conditionally sell their home to a newly created US government sponsored enterprise ("USHOMECORP") created by the FML in consideration of the benefits they will be receiving in a mortgage restructuring arrangement (a "Mortgage Restructuring Arrangement" or "MRA"). Where a home has multiple owners, a majority in interest of the owners must elect to participate for the home to be eligible for a MRA. Minority owners shall be bound by the actions of the majority owners.

4. The USHOMECORP shall be owned jointly by a newly created US government agency, which shall own the preferred stock for an investment of $1, and by private investors, which might include one or more of the currently existing entities which have been organized to buy and rent foreclosed homes, who shall purchase the common stock for an investment needed to adequately finance the entity. USHOMECORP shall be controlled and managed by a board of directors selected by the common stockholders but the US agency as preferred stockholder shall be entitled to representation on the board and shall have the right to take control under certain predetermined conditions. Jump Start America Bonds described herein might be used to partially finance USHOMECORP.

5. All MRAs shall be subject to a mortgage restructuring arrangement proceeding ("MRAP") brought jointly by the homeowner and USHOMECORP pursuant to a filing with and on a form prepared by the USMC. Prior to commencing a MRAP, USHOMECORP shall order and pay for appraisals of the FMV of the home from at least two qualified appraisers and a search of the outstanding liens against the home. The appraisers shall rely on standard appraisal techniques and valuation standards generally used in the neighborhood in which the home is located, but shall disregard sales prices of homes sold within the past two years in foreclosure proceedings or by a bank or other party after taking title to the property at a foreclosure proceeding or by a short sale in lieu of foreclosure.

6. The commencement of the MRAP shall automatically stay during the course of the MRAP all proceedings that may be pending or may be brought by mortgage or lien holders to foreclose against the property. Proceedings related to priority liens, such as local real estate tax sales, shall not

be affected by the MRAP except with the consent of the plaintiff in such proceeding.

7. The USHOMECORP shall thereafter make a preliminary determination of the FMV of the home that shall be not less than the lower of the appraisals. USHOMECORP shall also make its preliminary determination of the names and priorities of the lienholders that it may contact at its discretion. Such preliminary determinations shall be given to the homeowner together with copies of the appraisals and lien search. The homeowner shall have up to 20 days to notify the USHOMECORP that it either approves or disagrees with the USHOMECORP preliminary determination of the FMV of the property and if it disagrees, shall notify the USHOMECORP of its proposed alternative FMV of the property, which may be supported by an independent appraisal obtained and paid for by the homeowner. The USHOMECORP may accept the homeowner's preliminary valuation. Alternatively, the USHOMECORP may attempt to negotiate an agreed preliminary valuation with the homeowner prior to the commencement of the MRAP to attempt to reach an agreement with the homeowner on the preliminary FMV of the home which shall be not less that the lower of the appraisals obtained by USHOMECORP. The homeowner shall also advise USHOMECORP of any disagreement it may have relative to the liens.

8. The homeowner and the USHOMECORP shall then commence an MRAP in the USMC. After the filing of the MRAP, the USMC shall send a notice of the commencement of the MRAP to the USHOMECORP, the homeowner(s) and to all known lien holders together with the USHOMECORP's preliminary determination (as it may be modified after its negotiation with the homeowner) of the FMV of the home as well as the homeowner's proposed alternative FMV, if applicable, its preliminary determination of the names of

the lienholders and the amounts of the liens (including late fees and penalties) to the extent known and priorities of the liens, together with copies of the appraisals (including the homeowner's appraisal, if applicable) and a copy of the lien search and any written objections it has received from the homeowner relating to the liens. The notice shall be mailed by the USMC to all known interested parties at least 30 days prior to the hearing date determined by the USMC as set forth in the notice for the MRAP. Public notice of the commencement of the MRAP will be given within 10 days thereafter. All lienholders shall send at least ten days prior to the hearing date, proof of the amount (including late fees and penalties) of its liens to the USMC and all known parties.

9. The USMC shall hold a conference on the MRAP hearing date in an attempt to reach an agreement among all appearing parties as to the ownership of the property, the ownership, amount and priority of the liens and the FMV of the home. If such an agreement in not reached, the homeowner and any person claiming title or any mortgage or lienholder shall be entitled within 20 days after such hearing or such longer period as permitted by the USMC to submit to the USMC written opposition with supporting documents to the USHOMECORP's preliminary determination of the ownership, amount (including late fees and penalties) and priority of liens and the FMV of the home (which may include an appraisal) with proof of service of copies of such opposition documents to all parties who have entered an appearance in the proceeding. USHOMECORP, the homeowner and each mortgage or lien holder shall be given 10 additional days or such longer period as allowed by the USMC to reply to any other party's opposition to USHOMECORP's preliminary determination of the ownership of the property, ownership, amount and

priority of each mortgage or lien or FMV of the home. Copies of its reply shall be sent to all parties who have appeared in the proceeding.

10. The USMC shall then make a final determination as to ownership of the home, the amount owing on each mortgage and lien (including reasonable late fees and other obligations and penalties in accordance with the terms of the mortgage) and the priority of the creditors, the FMV of the home and the original owner rent equivalent payment (the "rent equivalent payment" or "REP" as hereafter defined.). The USMC shall have the authority under applicable state laws to determine ownership of the interests in liens where ownership is in question either as a result of poor documentation or conflicting claims to ownership of interest or principal payments and to determine the priority of existing liens.

11. The approved liens that are lowest in priority shall be reduced as necessary so that the aggregate amount of the approved liens will not exceed the FMV of the property. The USMC shall declare all liens that are subordinate to the approved liens equaling the FMV of the home to be voided in whole or in part and reduced or cancelled when the MRA is effective. If the aggregate of the approved liens do not exceed the FMV of the property, the amounts of the liens shall not be modified.

12. Liens prior to mortgage liens, such as liens for unpaid local taxes (including the portion of such lien which may accrue during the course of the MRAP), may be paid in full by USHOMECORP with interest and penalties during the course of but in any event shall be paid in full by USHOMECORP when the MRA becomes effective. The USHOMECORP shall upon making such payments become the owner of such priority liens. The homeowner shall be released from any

personal liability for any mortgage that remains in force when the MRA becomes effective and for any obligation extinguished during the course of the MRAP.

13. The USMC shall have the authority to order all mortgages to be modified to a standard mortgage created under the FML payable in equal monthly installments of interest and principal over a term of 30 years from the MRA effective date. The rate of interest for all mortgages should be a fair rate fixed at the termination of the MRAP as determined by Congress in the FML and modified from time to time in the manner determined by Congress to adjust for interest rate changes. To encourage and reward homeowners to stay current in their mortgage payments or RHPs prior to and during the pendency of the MRAP even though their mortgages are upside down or in default, the interest rate on the restructured mortgages of homeowners who have made a reasonable effort to remain current in all such payments until the end of the MRAP as determined by the USMC should be 1/4% less than the rate of interest on mortgages where the mortgage payments or RHPs have not been made by the homeowner.

14. Under the terms of the MRA, homeowners will be entitled to remain in the home and retain ownership by making a monthly REP to the USHOMECORP. The initial monthly REP shall equal the total of (i) principal and interest payments (the "Mortgage Payments") calculated to pay off all adjusted mortgages (the "Adjusted Mortgages") in constant monthly payments over a 30 year term at a fair interest rate and other terms as determined by Congress, (ii) 1/12 of the estimated aggregate amount of all RHPs which are incurred after the final determination in the MRAP including (a) real estate taxes and assessments, (b) coop, condo and association fees, (c) insurance costs and (d) water and sewer charges. A 5% late fee shall be added to each REP

payment that is not received by the USHOMECORP within ten days of the due date.

15. The Adjusted Mortgages shall in the aggregate equal the FMV of the home plus an adjustment (the "Priority Lien Adjustment"), if any. The Priority Lien Adjustment shall be an amount to be added to the FMV of the home when calculating the aggregate of the Adjusted Mortgages, which equals the payments owed by the homeowner and paid by the lien holders or USHOMECORP to local taxing authorities for property taxes or water and sewer rents and to condo and coop associations for past due maintenance payments unless such unpaid claims are or were subordinate to the lienholders whose liens aggregate the FMV of the home. The persons paying any priority lien shall receive a mortgage with a principal amount equal to the amounts paid by it to priority lienholders.

16. The homeowner shall during the course of the MRAP and at or prior to the hearing date set by the USMC deliver a valid deed in the name of USHOMECORP to an escrow agent selected by the USMC (the "Escrow Agent") The deed shall be in form as prepared by USHOMECORP to deliver title to USHOMECORP under local law. The homeowner shall also submit an affidavit at the commencement of the MRAP to the effect that the homeowner except as disclosed has not taken any actions to remove or permit the removal of any structural items and agrees not to do so during the course of the MRAP or during the term of the MRA. If any structural items have been removed by or with the consent of the homeowner, the homeowner shall agree to replace them within 90 days after the completion of the MRAP at his sole cost.

17. As a condition of its acceptance of the MRA, the homeowner shall pay the REP for the first month to USHOMECORP. The deed for the home in form to pass title to USHOMECORP in accordance with local law will continue to be held by the Escrow Agent subject to the terms of the MRA. The deed being held in escrow precludes the need for a security payment.

18. There shall be no change in ownership and no tax consequences to the homeowner when the deed is placed in escrow or if the deed is ultimately returned to the homeowner under the terms of the MRA. Nor shall there be any tax consequences to the homeowner as a result of the payment by the USHOMECORP of any mortgage payment or the forgiveness of principal or interest on the mortgage debt or any payments made by the USHOMECORP, if any, to third parties under the terms of the MRA to pay local taxes, condo, coop or association fees, insurance, or water or sewer charges relative to the home for obligations arising prior to or after the effectiveness of the MRA.

19. If the homeowner defaults and the deed being held in escrow is delivered by the Escrow Agent, subject to approval of the USMC, to the USHOMECORP, all filing and transfer fees shall be paid by USHOMECORP.

20. A lienholder whose lien is extinguished in whole or in part under the MRAP shall retain the right to receive payment for obligations that arise after the MRA becomes effective. For example, if a lien for condo or coop charges is reduced or extinguished in the MRA Proceeding, continuing condo, coop or association charges payable after the MRA becomes effective shall be treated as RHPs. The RHPs and therefore the REP will be adjusted from time to time to cover changes in real estate taxes, coop and condo association fees, insurance costs and water and sewer charges.

21. REPs made to USHOMECORP by the homeowner, to cover the mortgages and RHPs which would have been tax deductible if paid by the homeowner, shall be tax deductible at the time REPs are made as if they had been paid at such time directly by the homeowner to the third party who received such payments from USHOMECORP.

22. The homeowner shall realize his capital loss on the property if the deed and title is later transferred to USHOMECORP.

23. All oil, gas and electric utility charges shall be paid directly by the homeowner. All non-structural repairs, maintenance and non-structural replacements to the premises and repairs and replacements of the appliances, deck, patio, fencing, shrubbery, trees, pool and pool equipment and similar items shall be made by the homeowner at its sole cost and expense. All replacements of the heating, air conditioning and structural repairs and replacements as requested by the homeowner shall be paid by USHOMECORP. In such event, the homeowner shall obtain and submit at least two bids to USHOMECORP. USHOMECORP may approve one of the bids and hire and pay the contractor directly for the work or USHOMECORP may in its discretion reject both bids and solicit its own bid for the repair or replacement subject to the approval of the homeowner in its reasonable discretion. If the homeowner and USHOMECORP cannot agree on one of the bids, either the homeowner or USHOMECORP may request the USMC to select one of the bids at a hearing attended by both the homeowner and USHOMECORP. Such costs paid by USHOMECORP shall be treated as a new mortgage loan made by USHOMECORP to the homeowner and paid for by increasing the REP over the remaining term of the mortgages as same shall be extended in the reasonable discretion of USHOMECORP without reducing the monthly mortgage payments to the other mortgage holders.

24. USHOMECORP will guaranty the payment of all of the mortgages that remain in force as re-structured; provided that the amount of the guaranty shall not exceed 90% of the original principal amount of the mortgage as increased by Priority Lien Adjustments for amounts paid by the mortgage holder for the account of the homeowner. Under the terms of the MRA, USHOMECORP shall during the term of the MRA make all mortgage payments and the RHPs on behalf of the homeowner whether or not the homeowner pays the REPs. This will insure the mortgage holders that although the aggregate principal amount of the mortgages will be limited to the FMV of the home, future payments will be made on a timely basis. This will remove conflicts between the remaining mortgage holders and in some cases greatly enhance the value of subordinated mortgages. RHPs shall also be made by USHOMECORP on a timely basis subject to the right of the homeowner to contest at its expense the amount of any such RHP with the consent of USHOMECORP in its reasonable discretion.

25. The USHOMECORP shall notify the homeowner each time the REP is adjusted and provide the homeowner with the basis for such adjustment.

26. Either the homeowner or the USHOMECORP may commence a certiorari proceeding to contest any property tax increase or assessment. The reasonable costs incurred in accordance with local practice in connection with any such proceeding shall be paid only out of the recovery and the REP shall be equitably adjusted based on the outcome of the proceeding.

27. MOST IMPORTANTLY, homeowners entering into a MRA with USHOMECORP will have an option to recover the deed from the Escrow Agent during the term of the MRA by paying an escrow release price (the "Escrow Release

Price"). However, as a condition to the release of the deed from Escrow, the homeowner or his successor in interest shall be required to obtain a release of the guaranty of USHOMECORP on all mortgages by refinancing or repaying all outstanding mortgages.

28. The Escrow Release Price shall be an amount that enables the USHOMECORP to recover all out of pocket payments made from time to time after the commencement of the MRAP and during the MRA including all mortgages held by USHOMECORP (or to which it is entitled), all other mortgage payments, state and local taxes, condo and coop fees, insurance costs and water and sewer fees, net of REPs received from the homeowner and earn a predetermined profit percentage (1-2%) on such net out of pocket payments. A large percentage of such items will be included in the REPs with the result that in cases where the homeowner has made all the REPs the Escrow Release price will be small unless the homeowner has failed to make the RHPs due prior to the conclusion of the MRAP or substantial structural repairs and replacements have been made. The USHOMECORP shall annually notify the homeowner the amount of the adjusted Escrow Release Price. The Escrow Release Price will rise during grace periods when the homeowner is not paying the REPs and the USHOMECORP is paying the mortgages and the RHPs.

29. Homeowners with underwater mortgages who remain current in their RHPs will be able to avail themselves of a new MRAP after a 5-year period to further reduce the mortgages if circumstances warrant.

30. To encourage owners to elect to commence a MRAP before knowing the final decision of the USMC, the homeowner shall be entitled to elect to terminate and rescind the MRAP at any time prior to 10 days after the USMC has

rendered its final decision in the MRAP on notice to the USMC and payment to the USHOMECORP of all funds it has paid to third parties on behalf of the homeowner such as property taxes or coop, condo or association fees in accordance with the terms of the MRAP. USHOMECORP shall then give notice of termination of the MRAP to all parties who have appeared in the proceeding. To prevent the use of an MRAP as a delaying tactic by the homeowner, any mortgagee or lienholder will have the right within 20 days after notice that the homeowner has terminated the MRAP to request the USMC to retain jurisdiction over all parties who have appeared in the MRAP and convert the MRAP into a foreclosure proceeding which shall be enforced under state law. A homeowner who terminates a MRAP shall not be able to seek a later MRA for a period of at least two years without the consent of the USHOMECORP that may be withheld in its reasonable discretion.

31. The USMC will have the power to conclusively determine in the MRAP who the owner of the home is who qualifies to participate in the MRA. The USMC will also have the exclusive power to determine the FMV of the home and the existence, ownership and priorities of existing liens in an amount not to exceed the FMV of the home plus the amount of the Priority Lien Adjustment. The USMC shall respect the property rights and priorities of lien holders but shall have the power of a bankruptcy court to give debt relief from terminated or reduced liens.

32. The effectiveness of the MRA need not be delayed pending the final determination of the ownership or the amounts or priorities of the existing liens. The aggregate of the mortgage payments based on the FMV of the home as determined by the USMC shall be paid by USHOMECORP to the appropriate mortgage holders upon the final decision of the USMC.

33. The homeowner (or his successors in interest) may, if current in making its REPs, on 10 days prior notice given to the USHOMECORP a) sell or otherwise transfer his right to regain possession of the deed being held in Escrow under the MRA to a successor in interest who agrees to assume the obligations of the homeowner and be subject to the terms and conditions of the MRA or b) lease the home to a third party. This would enable the homeowner to realize a benefit from the equity that may develop in the home.

34. A potential buyer of the homeowner's interest will be able with homeowner's consent to ascertain from the USHOMECORP whether the homeowner is current in making his REPs. Because of the low downside risk to a buyer who will be purchasing the homeowner's interest subject to mortgages, which at the conclusion of the MRAP aggregated the FMV of the home as increased by any Priority Lien Adjustment, a homeowner who had not defaulted prior to the MRAP in making his RHPs can expect that his home will have a small equity value immediately upon the completion of the MRAP. Such equity will increase over time if the housing market recovers and the REPs are paid.

35. The USMC shall retain jurisdiction to determine whether the homeowner has defaulted under the terms of the MRA entitling the USHOMECORP to obtain possession of the deed from the Escrow Agent and file the deed transferring ownership of the home to the USHOMECORP. It shall have authority to resolve any dispute between the homeowner and USHOMECORP over (i) the right of the homeowner to exercise its option to obtain the deed from the Escrow Agent, (ii) the Escrow Release Price (iii) as to payment of the Escrow Release Price (iv) the amount of the REP adjustments and the payment of the REPs and (v) any

other dispute between the homeowner or its assignees and USHOMECORP relating to the MRA.

36. To discourage homeowners from electing a MRA and defaulting shortly after the MRA is approved there shall during the first year after the MRA is approved be a short 30 day default period following notice to the homeowner of the failure to pay a monthly REP. After such 30 day period USHOMECORP shall send notice to the homeowner and the USMC that homeowner is in default in payment of the REP. The homeowner shall have 30 days to cure such default.

37. A homeowner who voluntarily terminates the MRA and agrees that the deed may be transferred to the USHOMECORP or is found in a summary proceeding held before the USMC to be in default in making the REPs not cured prior to the date of the default proceeding or such extended period as may be allowed by the USMC, will lose its right to retain ownership of or live in the premises. In such event, the Escrow Agent at the direction of the USMC shall deliver the deed to USHOMECORP, which shall upon the filing of the deed in accordance with local law become the owner of the home and be entitled to a obtain a summary eviction of the homeowner on petition to the USMC.

38. After the first year the homeowner shall be entitled to a 60-day cure period. Moreover, to protect homeowners who have over time reduced the principal amount of the mortgages or who suffer a short term hardship from losing their home, homeowners will be given an option beginning one year after the commencement of the MRA which shall automatically be deemed to be exercised to add a defined number of REPs not in excess of one REP during each of the next three years nor in excess of an aggregate of six REPs